UK Ninja Dual Zone Air Fryer Cookbook 2024

Super Easy and Healthy Ninja Foodi Recipes for Beginners to Make Most of Your Double Zone Air Fryer | Full Colour Edition

Brianna C. Self

Copyright© 2024 By Brianna C. Self
All Rights Reserved

This book is copyright protected. It is only for personal use.
You cannot amend, distribute, sell, use,
quote or paraphrase any part of the content within this book,
without the consent of the author or publisher.
Under no circumstances will any blame or
legal responsibility be held against the publisher,
or author, for any damages, reparation,
or monetary loss due to the information contained within this book,
either directly or indirectly.

Disclaimer Notice:

Please note the information contained within this
document is for educational and entertainment purposes only.
All effort has been executed to present accurate,
up to date, reliable, complete information.
No warranties of any kind are declared or implied.
Readers acknowledge that the author is not engaged
in the rendering of legal,
financial, medical or professional advice.
The content within this book has been derived from various sources.
Please consult a licensed professional before attempting any
techniques outlined in this book.
By reading this document,
the reader agrees that under no circumstances is the
author responsible for any losses,
direct or indirect,
that are incurred as a result of the use of the
information contained within this document, including,
but not limited to, errors, omissions, or inaccuracies.

Contents

Chapter 1: All About the Ninja Dual Zone 1

Chapter 2: About the Recipes 6

CHAPTER 3: Breakfast Recipes 8

CHAPTER 4: Main Recipes 14

CHAPTER 5: Fish and Seafood 23

CHAPTER 6 : Poultry and Meat Recipes 32

CHAPTER 7: Beans and Legumes 41

CHAPTER 8: Healthy Vegetables and Sides 50

CHAPTER 9: Family Favourites 59

CHAPTER 10: Appetisers 68

CHAPTER 11: Sweet Snacks and Desserts 74

INDEX 80

Chapter 1: All About the Ninja Dual Zone

In the bustling kitchens of the United Kingdom, where time and budget often dictate our culinary choices, the Ninja Dual Zone Air Fryer emerges as the unsung hero, transforming ordinary meals into extraordinary feasts without breaking the bank. We're thrilled to present our collection of budget-friendly recipes that embrace the versatility of the Ninja Dual Zone Air Fryer, ensuring that delicious and affordable meals are just a button press away.

As we navigate the culinary landscape, we understand the need for practicality without compromising on taste. This cookbook is a celebration of smart cooking—where innovation meets affordability. Whether you're a student trying to master the art of cooking on a tight budget or a family looking for quick, nutritious, and wallet-friendly meals, this book is your go-to guide for maximising the potential of your air fryer.

Inside these pages, you'll discover a treasure trove of recipes designed to tantalise your taste buds and simplify your cooking routine. From breakfast to dinner and everything in between, we've curated a diverse selection of recipes that cater to a range of tastes and preferences. The Ninja Dual Zone Air Fryer becomes your culinary accomplice, effortlessly producing crispy textures, succulent flavours, and meals that won't leave your wallet gasping for breath.

What sets this book apart is its unwavering commitment to affordability without compromising on quality. We've meticulously crafted each recipe to include readily available ingredients, ensuring that you won't need to scour speciality stores or sacrifice your hard-earned pounds for gourmet delights. Every dish in this cookbook embodies the essence of home-cooked comfort, infused with the modern twist that the Ninja Dual Zone Air Fryer effortlessly brings to your kitchen.

Get ready to embark on a culinary journey that is not only delicious but also friendly to your pocket. This book is more than a cookbook; it's a companion for those seeking the perfect balance between taste, budget, and convenience. Let's redefine home cooking together and make every meal an affordable masterpiece. Happy cooking!

Why Choose the Ninja Dual Zone Air Fryer?
In the realm of kitchen appliances, the Ninja Dual Zone Air Fryer stands as a game-changer, and here's why it deserves a prime spot in your culinary arsenal:

Dual Zone Technology: The Ninja Dual Zone Air Fryer isn't your average kitchen gadget—it's a multitasking marvel. With its innovative dual-zone technology, you can now cook two different dishes simultaneously without flavour mingling. Imagine sizzling chicken wings on one side and golden fries on the other, all harmoniously reaching perfection at the same time.

Precision at Your Fingertips: Tailor your cooking experience with precision control. The Ninja Dual Zone Air Fryer allows you to set independent temperatures and cooking times for each zone, ensuring that diverse ingredients receive the exact treatment they deserve. Whether you're crisping up veggies or baking desserts, you're in command of your culinary destiny.

Versatile Cooking Options: Say goodbye to monotony in your meals. This air fryer doesn't limit itself to frying alone. Roast, bake, dehydrate, and reheat with finesse. The versatility of the Ninja Dual Zone Air Fryer adds a new dimension to your kitchen, allowing you to explore a myriad of cooking techniques with just one appliance.

Healthier Cooking, Less Guilt: Achieve that coveted crispiness with up to 75% less fat compared to traditional frying methods. The Ninja Dual Zone Air Fryer promotes a healthier lifestyle without compromising on flavour. Indulge in your favourite dishes guilt-free, knowing that your culinary creations are prepared with a touch of wellness.

Time-Efficient and Energy-Saving: The pace of modern life demands efficiency, and the Ninja Dual Zone Air Fryer delivers. Quick preheating and rapid cooking times mean your meals are ready in a fraction of the time it would take using conventional methods. Save not only time but also energy, as this appliance is designed to be as economical as it is practical.

Easy Cleanup, More Enjoyment: Nobody enjoys spending more time cleaning up than actually relishing a delicious meal. The Ninja Dual Zone Air Fryer is designed with your convenience in mind. Non-stick surfaces, dishwasher-safe accessories, and a hassle-free cleanup process ensure that your post-cooking ritual is as enjoyable as the cooking itself.

Make the Ninja Dual Zone Air Fryer your kitchen companion, and embark on a culinary adventure where convenience, versatility, and precision converge to elevate your cooking experience. Whether you're a seasoned chef or a cooking novice, this appliance is the key to unlocking a world of flavours without breaking the bank. Welcome to a new era of affordable, efficient, and delectable cooking!

The Benefits of Using the Ninja Dual Zone
Discover a world of culinary possibilities with the Ninja Dual Zone Air Fryer—a kitchen companion that transcends the ordinary. Here are the remarkable benefits that make this appliance a must-have for every home cook:

Dual-Zone Cooking Brilliance: Embrace the freedom to cook two different dishes simultaneously. With its innovative dual-zone technology, the Ninja Dual Zone Air Fryer allows you to independently control the cooking settings for each zone. Say goodbye to the limitations of a single-zone air fryer and welcome the flexibility of a culinary marvel.

Time-Saving Efficiency: In the fast-paced

rhythm of modern life, efficiency is key. The Ninja Dual Zone Air Fryer not only cooks your favourite meals with precision but does so in record time. Say farewell to lengthy cooking sessions, and enjoy delicious, crispy results in a fraction of the time it would take with traditional methods.

Versatility at Your Fingertips: Unleash your creativity in the kitchen with the Ninja Dual Zone's versatile cooking options. From air frying and roasting to baking and dehydrating, this appliance is a true all-in-one powerhouse. It adapts to your culinary ambitions, making it a versatile solution for breakfast, lunch, dinner, and everything in between.

Healthier, Crispy Results: Indulge in your favourite fried delights guilt-free. The Ninja Dual Zone Air Fryer lets you enjoy the crispy texture you love with up to 75% less fat compared to traditional frying methods. Health-conscious cooking has never been this satisfying.

Precision Temperature Control: Take control of your cooking with precise temperature settings. Whether you're searing, baking, or dehydrating, the Ninja Dual Zone Air Fryer empowers you with the exact temperatures needed for optimal results. Achieve culinary perfection with every dish.

Family-Friendly Convenience: Cooking for the whole family has never been easier. The spacious cooking capacity of the Ninja Dual Zone ensures that you can whip up generous portions in one go, saving you time and energy. Say goodbye to juggling multiple batches and hello to stress-free family meals.

Easy-to-Clean Design: Enjoy the benefits of hassle-free maintenance. The Ninja Dual Zone Air Fryer is designed with easy cleanup in mind. Removable, dishwasher-safe accessories and non-stick surfaces make post-cooking cleanup a breeze, leaving you with more time to savour your culinary creations.

Energy-Efficient Operation: Contribute to a greener planet while enjoying your favourite meals. The Ninja Dual Zone Air Fryer is designed to be energy-efficient, reducing your carbon footprint while delivering outstanding cooking performance.

Elevate your culinary experience and transform the way you cook with the Ninja Dual Zone Air Fryer. From efficiency and versatility to healthier outcomes, this kitchen dynamo is your ticket to a world of delectable possibilities. Get ready to reimagine your cooking journey—one delicious meal at a time!

How to Clean and Maintain Your Air Fryer

Congratulations on bringing the versatile Ninja Dual Zone Air Fryer into your kitchen. To ensure it continues to deliver mouthwatering meals, it's essential to keep it clean and well-maintained. Follow these simple steps for easy and effective cleaning:

Cool Down Before Cleaning: Always allow your Ninja Dual Zone Air Fryer to cool down before cleaning. Unplug the appliance and give it a few minutes to reach a safe temperature.

Detach and Wash Accessories: Remove the cooking basket, crisper plate, and any other accessories from the air fryer. These components are usually dishwasher-safe, making cleanup a breeze. Alternatively, wash them with warm, soapy water and a non-abrasive sponge for quick hand cleaning.

Wipe Down the Interior: Using a damp cloth or sponge, gently wipe down the interior of the air fryer. Be sure to remove any food residue or oil that may have accumulated during cooking. If necessary, a mild detergent can be used, but avoid harsh chemicals that may damage the non-stick surfaces.

Clean the Heating Element: Occasionally, check the heating element for any buildup. If you notice residue, use a soft brush or cloth to gently remove it. Be cautious not to scratch or damage the heating element during this process.

Exterior Maintenance: Wipe down the exterior of

the air fryer with a damp cloth to remove any grease or stains. For stainless steel surfaces, a mild stainless steel cleaner can be used to restore shine. Always ensure the appliance is unplugged before cleaning the exterior.

Regular Deep Cleaning: For every few uses, consider a more thorough cleaning. Remove the drip tray and check for any excess oil or debris. Clean the interior and exterior with extra attention to detail, ensuring a spotless appliance.

Avoid Abrasive Cleaners: Steer clear of abrasive sponges, scouring pads, or harsh cleaning agents, as they can damage the non-stick coating and other surfaces of your air fryer. Opt for soft materials to maintain the longevity of your appliance.

Store Properly: When not in use, store your air fryer in a cool, dry place. Ensure proper ventilation to prevent any odours from lingering.

By following these straightforward steps, you'll not only keep your Ninja Dual Zone Air Fryer in top-notch condition but also guarantee that each meal is as delicious and healthy as the last.

Air Fryer Tips and Tricks

Unlock the full potential of your culinary adventure with these invaluable tips and tricks for mastering the art of air frying with the Ninja Dual Zone. Whether you're a seasoned chef or a kitchen novice, these insights will elevate your air frying experience to new heights:

Preheat for Success: Just like conventional ovens, preheating your air fryer is key to achieving that perfect crispiness. Give it a few minutes to reach the desired temperature before placing your ingredients for optimal results.

Pat Dry Ingredients: For a crisper texture, pat dry ingredients like meats and vegetables before placing them in the air fryer. Removing excess moisture ensures that the hot air can work its magic more efficiently.

Embrace the Oil Mist: Instead of traditional frying, use an oil mist or a cooking spray to lightly coat your ingredients. This minimal amount of oil enhances the crispiness without sacrificing the health benefits of air frying.

Single-Layer Mastery: To ensure even cooking, arrange your ingredients in a single layer. This allows the hot air to circulate freely, resulting in consistent and delightful outcomes.

Shake and Flip Technique: Midway through the cooking process, shake or flip your ingredients. This ensures that every side gets its fair share of crispy perfection. It's the secret to achieving an all-around delightful texture.

Temperature Precision: Familiarise yourself with the recommended temperatures for different foods. Higher temperatures are ideal for items that need a quick, crispy finish, while lower temperatures work well for delicate items or dehydrating.

Mix and Match Flavors: Experiment with seasonings and marinades to add a burst of flavour to your dishes. The air fryer enhances the infusion of spices, herbs, and marinades, making your meals a culinary sensation.

Don't Overcrowd: While it's tempting to maximise the cooking space, overcrowding can hinder air circulation. Opt for smaller batches to ensure each item cooks to perfection.

Keep an Eye on Texture: Monitor your food as it cooks. Air frying can be quick, and checking on your ingredients ensures they reach the desired level of crispiness without crossing into overcooked territory.

Clean Regularly: A well-maintained air fryer performs at its best. Regularly clean the removable parts, such as the cooking basket and crisper plate, to keep your appliance in top-notch condition.

Explore the Dual Zone: Take advantage of the Ninja Dual Zone's unique feature. Experiment with cooking different items in each zone simultaneously, expanding your culinary repertoire and saving time.

Armed with these air fryer tips and tricks, you're ready to embark on a flavorful journey with your Ninja Dual Zone Air Fryer. Whether you're aiming for a quick snack or a family feast, these insights will ensure your air-frying adventures are a resounding success.

FAQs

Q1: Can I cook frozen food directly in the air fryer?

Answer: Absolutely! One of the perks of using the air fryer is its ability to cook frozen foods without the need for thawing. Just adjust the cooking time and temperature according to the air fryer's guidelines for frozen items.

Q2: Is it safe to use cooking spray in the air fryer?

Answer: Yes, it's safe to use cooking spray, but opt for an oil mist or a light coating. Be cautious not to use aerosol cooking sprays with propellants, as they can damage the non-stick coating over time. A manual pump or brush-style sprayer is a better choice.

Q3: Can I bake in the air fryer, or is it just for frying?

Answer: The Ninja Dual Zone Air Fryer is incredibly versatile. Besides frying, you can bake, roast, dehydrate, and more. It's an all-in-one kitchen workhorse that opens the door to a variety of cooking possibilities.

Q4: How do I prevent my food from sticking to the air fryer basket?

Answer: To prevent sticking, lightly coat the food with oil or use a non-stick cooking spray. Additionally, make sure the food is arranged in a single layer, allowing proper air circulation for even cooking.

Q5: What is the purpose of the dual-zone feature, and how do I use it effectively?

Answer: The dual-zone feature allows you to cook two different dishes simultaneously, each with its own set of cooking parameters. To use it effectively, ensure that the foods being cooked together have similar cooking times and temperature requirements. This feature is a game-changer for multitasking in the kitchen.

Q6: Can I use aluminium foil in the air fryer basket?

Answer: Yes, you can use aluminium foil, but be sure to follow the air fryer's guidelines. Do not completely cover the basket, as it may hinder air circulation. Instead, create a loose foil packet or shape the foil to allow air to flow freely.

Q7: How do I clean the heating element safely?

Answer: Gently clean the heating element with a soft brush or cloth. Be cautious not to damage or scratch it during the cleaning process. Always ensure the air fryer is unplugged and has cooled down before attempting to clean the heating element.

Q8: Can I cook raw meat and vegetables together in the air fryer?

Answer: Yes, you can cook raw meat and vegetables together. However, consider the required cooking times for each item. If they have significantly different cooking times, you might want to start cooking the one that takes longer and add the other later in the process.

These FAQs are designed to address common queries about the Ninja Dual Zone Air Fryer. If you have more specific questions, consult the user manual or reach out to the Ninja customer support team for personalised assistance.

Chapter 2: About the Recipes

In the hustle and bustle of our daily lives, we've all become acutely aware of the rising costs that seem to touch every aspect of our existence. As we navigate the twists and turns of budgeting, the desire for delicious, home-cooked meals remains unwavering. It is with this understanding and a touch of empathy that we present to you a culinary haven — a collection of recipes crafted not only for their mouth watering flavours but also for their pocket-friendly appeal.

In the United Kingdom, where every pound counts, we feel the pinch of the escalating cost of living. Yet, the joy of a good meal need not be sacrificed on the altar of expenses. Hence, we've curated a selection of recipes that embrace simplicity, affordability, and, most importantly, ease of preparation. We acknowledge the challenges many face in today's economic climate, and our goal is to empower you to create delicious meals without burdening your budget.

These recipes are more than a compilation of ingredients and instructions; they are a culinary embrace, inviting you to rediscover the joy of home cooking without the stress of overspending. Each dish is a testament to the notion that affordability can coexist harmoniously with taste, and that a satisfying meal need not be synonymous with financial strain.

Whether you're a student diligently watching your expenses or a family navigating the intricacies of the monthly budget, our collection of affordable and easy-to-make recipes is designed to be your ally in the kitchen. We believe that everyone deserves the pleasure of a home-cooked meal, and it is our sincere hope that these recipes bring not just sustenance but a sense of joy, comfort, and accomplishment to your table.

So, let's embark on this culinary journey together — a journey that appreciates the economic challenges we face and transforms them into an opportunity for creativity and flavour. Here's to making delicious memories without breaking the bank, one affordable and easy recipe at a time.

How to Cut Costs in the Kitchen

In the face of rising living costs, the kitchen can become a battlefield for budget-conscious individuals seeking to balance the desire for delicious meals with the necessity of fiscal responsibility. Fear not, aspiring home chefs, for there are myriad ways to cut costs in the kitchen without sacrificing flavour or nutrition. Here's a practical guide to help you navigate the culinary world while keeping your wallet intact:

Embrace Seasonal Produce: Opt for fruits and vegetables that are in season. Not only are they fresher, but they are also more affordable. Seasonal produce tends to be abundant, driving prices down and allowing you to incorporate a variety of flavours into your meals.

Master the Art of Meal Planning: Planning your meals in advance not only reduces food waste but also prevents unnecessary trips to the grocery store. Create a weekly meal plan, make a shopping list, and stick to it. This not only saves money but also ensures you have all the necessary ingredients on hand.

Buy in Bulk: Certain pantry staples, like rice, pasta, and legumes, can be purchased in bulk, saving you money in the long run. Keep an eye out for sales and discounts on non-perishable items, and stock up when the prices are low.

Emphasise Plant-Based Proteins: Incorporating more plant-based proteins into your meals, such as beans, lentils, and tofu, can be both cost-effective and healthy. These alternatives often cost less than their meat counterparts and can be just as satisfying.

Limit Convenience Foods: While convenient, pre-packaged and processed foods often come with a higher price tag. Invest time in preparing meals from scratch, as this not only reduces costs but also allows you to control the quality of ingredients.

Minimise Food Waste: Be mindful of expiration dates and organise your fridge and pantry to ensure that nothing gets lost in the abyss. Consider repurposing leftovers into new dishes to extend their life and minimise waste.

Explore Discount Stores: Don't overlook discount stores and local markets. They often offer quality ingredients at lower prices than larger supermarkets. Keep an open mind, and you might discover hidden gems that align with both your taste buds and your budget.

DIY Kitchen Staples: Instead of purchasing pre-made sauces and dressings, try making them at home. Not only is this more cost-effective, but it also allows you to tailor flavours to your liking and avoid unnecessary additives.

Take Advantage of Sales and Coupons: Keep an eye on sales, discounts, and coupons for both online and local grocery stores. Planning your shopping around promotions can significantly reduce your overall grocery bill.

Cook in Batches and Freeze: Prepare larger quantities of meals and freeze individual portions. This not only saves you time in the long run but also prevents the temptation of ordering takeout on busy days.

By incorporating these cost-cutting strategies into your culinary routine, you'll find that preparing delicious and budget-friendly meals becomes a satisfying and rewarding endeavour. Empower yourself in the kitchen, and let the joy of cooking coexist harmoniously with financial prudence.

CHAPTER 3
Breakfast Recipes

Crispy Air-Fried Bubble and Squeak Patties

Serves: 4
Prep time: 10 minutes
Cook time: 15 minutes

Ingredients:
- 500g mashed potatoes
- 100g carrots, grated
- 2 cloves garlic, minced
- 1 large egg
- Salt and black pepper, to taste
- Cooking spray or oil for brushing
- 200g cabbage, finely shredded
- 1 onion, finely chopped
- 2 tbsp plain flour

Preparation instructions:
1. Preheat the Ninja Dual Zone Air Fryer to 200°C for 5 minutes.
2. In a large mixing bowl, combine the mashed potatoes, shredded cabbage, grated carrots, chopped onion, minced garlic, plain flour, and the beaten egg.
3. Season the mixture with salt and black pepper to taste, ensuring even distribution.
4. Form the mixture into patties, ensuring they are compact and well-shaped.
5. Place the patties in the Ninja Dual Zone Air Fryer basket, leaving space between each for optimal air circulation.
6. Air fry at 200°C for 15-18 minutes or until the patties are golden brown and crispy, flipping halfway through the cooking time.
7. Once done, remove from the air fryer and let them cool slightly before serving.

English Muffin Egg Cups with Turkey Sausage

Serves: 4
Prep time: 10 minutes
Cook time: 15 minutes

Ingredients:
- 4 whole wheat English muffins, split and toasted
- 200g turkey sausage, cooked and crumbled
- 4 large eggs
- 60ml skimmed milk
- 50g shredded mozzarella cheese
- Fresh chives, chopped, for garnish
- Salt and black pepper, to taste

Preparation instructions:
1. Preheat the Ninja Dual Zone Air Fryer to 180°C for 5 minutes.
2. Place each English muffin half in a silicone muffin cup.
3. Distribute the cooked and crumbled turkey sausage equally among the muffin cups.
4. In a bowl, whisk together the eggs, skimmed milk, shredded mozzarella, salt, and black pepper.
5. Pour the egg mixture into each muffin cup until it reaches the top.
6. Air fry at 180°C for 12-15 minutes or until the eggs are set and the tops are lightly browned.
7. Garnish with chopped fresh chives and serve warm.

Air-Fried Veggie Hash Browns Delight

Serves: 4
Prep time: 10 minutes
Cook time: 15 minutes

Ingredients:
- 500g grated sweet potatoes
- 100g grated courgette, excess moisture squeezed out
- 1 red pepper, finely diced
- 1 small onion, finely chopped
- 2 tbsp olive oil
- 1 tsp smoked paprika
- 1/2 tsp garlic powder
- Salt and black pepper, to taste

Preparation instructions:
1. Preheat the Ninja Dual Zone Air Fryer to 190°C for 5 minutes.
2. In a large bowl, combine the grated sweet potatoes, squeezed courgette, diced red pepper, chopped onion, olive oil, smoked paprika, garlic powder, salt, and black pepper.
3. Mix the ingredients thoroughly until well combined.
4. Form the mixture into patties and place them in the Ninja Dual Zone Air Fryer basket.
5. Air fry at 190°C for 15-18 minutes or until the hash browns are crispy and golden brown, flipping halfway through.
6. Once cooked, remove from the air fryer and let them cool for a few minutes before serving.

Cheesy Beans on Toast Twists

Serves: 4
Prep time: 10 minutes
Cook time: 15 minutes

Ingredients:
- 400g canned baked beans
- 100g grated cheddar cheese
- 4 slices whole-grain bread
- 2 tbsp butter, melted
- 1 tsp dried mixed herbs
- Salt and black pepper, to taste

Preparation instructions:
1. Preheat the Ninja Dual Zone Air Fryer to 180°C for 5 minutes.
2. In a bowl, combine the baked beans, grated cheddar cheese, dried mixed herbs, salt, and black pepper.
3. Cut the whole-grain bread into smaller pieces or use a cookie cutter for fun shapes.
4. Brush each bread piece with melted butter on both sides.
5. Place the bread in the air fryer basket and air fry at 180°C for 5 minutes or until golden brown and crispy.
6. Spoon the cheesy baked beans mixture onto the toasted bread.
7. Air fry for an additional 5-8 minutes until the cheese is melted and bubbly.
8. Once done, remove from the air fryer and serve the Cheesy Beans on Toast Twists hot.

Spinach and Feta Stuffed Mushrooms

Serves: 4
Prep time: 15 minutes
Cook time: 12 minutes

Ingredients:
- 300g large mushrooms, stems removed and chopped
- 100g fresh spinach, chopped
- 75g feta cheese, crumbled
- 2 tbsp olive oil
- 2 cloves garlic, minced
- 1 tsp dried oregano
- Salt and black pepper, to taste

Preparation instructions:
1. Preheat the Ninja Dual Zone Air Fryer to 190°C for 5 minutes.
2. In a pan, heat olive oil over medium heat. Add chopped mushroom stems, minced garlic, and cook until softened.
3. Add chopped spinach to the pan and cook until wilted.
4. Remove the pan from heat and stir in crumbled feta, dried oregano, salt, and black pepper.
5. Stuff each mushroom cap with the spinach and feta mixture.
6. Place the stuffed mushrooms in the air fryer basket and air fry at 190°C for 12 minutes or until the mushrooms are tender.
7. Once done, remove from the air fryer and let them cool slightly before serving.

Ninja Dual Zone Full English Breakfast Bites

Serves: 4
Prep time: 15 minutes
Cook time: 20 minutes

Ingredients:
- 8 pork sausages, cooked and chopped
- 4 large eggs
- 200g cherry tomatoes, halved
- 100g button mushrooms, sliced
- 4 slices black pudding, chopped
- 1 tbsp olive oil
- Salt and black pepper, to taste
- Fresh parsley, chopped, for garnish

Preparation instructions:
1. Preheat the Ninja Dual Zone Air Fryer to 180°C for 5 minutes.
2. In a pan, heat olive oil over medium heat. Add chopped black pudding, sliced mushrooms, and halved cherry tomatoes. Cook until vegetables are softened.
3. Add the cooked and chopped pork sausages to the pan and mix well.
4. Spoon the sausage and vegetable mixture evenly into four silicone muffin cups.
5. Crack a large egg over the top of each cup.
6. Place the muffin cups in the air fryer basket and air fry at 180°C for 18-20 minutes or until the eggs are set.
7. Garnish with chopped fresh parsley and serve the Ninja Zone Full English Breakfast Bites hot.

Sweet Potato Rosti with Avocado Smash

Serves: 4
Prep time: 15 minutes
Cook time: 20 minutes

Ingredients:
- 500g sweet potatoes, peeled and grated
- 1 onion, finely chopped
- 2 tbsp olive oil
- Salt and black pepper, to taste
- 2 ripe avocados
- 1 tbsp lemon juice
- Chilli flakes, for garnish
- Fresh coriander, chopped, for garnish

Preparation instructions:
1. Preheat the Ninja Dual Zone Air Fryer to 190°C for 5 minutes.
2. In a bowl, combine the grated sweet potatoes, chopped onion, olive oil, salt, and black pepper.
3. Form the mixture into rosti patties and place them in the air fryer basket.
4. Air fry at 190°C for 15-18 minutes or until the sweet potato rosti is golden brown and crispy, flipping halfway through.
5. While the rosti cooks, mash the ripe avocados in a bowl, add lemon juice, and season with salt and black pepper to taste.
6. Once the rosti is cooked, serve it with a generous dollop of avocado smash.
7. Garnish with chilli flakes and fresh coriander before serving.

Mushroom and Tomato Breakfast Quesadillas

Serves: 4
Prep time: 10 minutes
Cook time: 15 minutes

Ingredients:
- 200g mushrooms, sliced
- 200g cherry tomatoes, quartered
- 1 red onion, thinly sliced
- 1 tbsp olive oil
- Salt and black pepper, to taste
- 4 large whole wheat tortillas
- 200g shredded mozzarella cheese
- 4 large eggs
- Fresh parsley, chopped, for garnish

Preparation instructions:
1. Preheat the Ninja Dual Zone Air Fryer to 180°C for 5 minutes.
2. In a pan, heat olive oil over medium heat. Add sliced mushrooms, quartered cherry tomatoes, and thinly sliced red onion. Cook until the vegetables are softened.
3. Season the mixture with salt and black pepper to taste.
4. Lay out the whole wheat tortillas and sprinkle shredded mozzarella cheese evenly on one half of each tortilla.
5. Spoon the mushroom and tomato mixture over the cheese, dividing it equally among the tortillas.
6. Fold the tortillas in half, creating quesadillas.
7. Place the quesadillas in the air fryer basket and air fry at 180°C for 10-12 minutes or until the cheese is melted and the tortillas are crispy.
8. While the quesadillas cook, fry the eggs in a pan until the whites are set but the yolks are still runny.
9. Once the quesadillas are done, top each with a fried egg.
10. Garnish with chopped fresh parsley before serving.

Banana-Oat Pancake Bites with Yoghurt Drizzle

Serves: 4
Prep time: 15 minutes
Cook time: 12 minutes

Ingredients:
- 2 ripe bananas, mashed
- 1 large egg
- 1 tsp vanilla extract
- 1/2 tsp ground cinnamon
- Cooking spray
- 2 tbsp honey
- 100g rolled oats
- 60ml milk
- 1 tsp baking powder
- Pinch of salt
- 150g Greek yoghurt
- Fresh berries, for garnish

Preparation instructions:
1. Preheat the Ninja Dual Zone Air Fryer to 180°C for 5 minutes.
2. In a bowl, combine mashed bananas, rolled oats, egg, milk, vanilla extract, baking powder, ground cinnamon, and a pinch of salt. Mix well.
3. Grease the silicone muffin cups with cooking spray.
4. Divide the banana-oat mixture equally among 4 muffin cups.
5. Place the muffin cups in the air fryer basket and air fry at 180°C for 10-12 minutes or until the pancake bites are set and lightly golden.
6. While the pancake bites cool, mix Greek yoghurt and honey in a bowl.
7. Drizzle the yoghurt mixture over the pancake bites.
8. Garnish with fresh berries and serve.

Mediterranean Chickpea Frittatas in the Air Fryer

Serves: 4
Prep time: 20 minutes
Cook time: 15 minutes

Ingredients:
- 400g canned chickpeas, drained and rinsed
- 4 large eggs
- 60ml olive oil
- 1 red pepper, diced
- 1 red onion, finely chopped
- 100g cherry tomatoes, halved
- 50g feta cheese, crumbled
- 1 tsp dried oregano
- Salt and black pepper, to taste
- Fresh parsley, chopped, for garnish

Preparation instructions:
1. Preheat the Ninja Dual Zone Air Fryer to 190°C for 5 minutes.
2. In a food processor, blend chickpeas, eggs, and olive oil until smooth.
3. In a bowl, mix the chickpea mixture with diced red pepper, finely chopped red onion, halved cherry tomatoes, crumbled feta, dried oregano, salt, and black pepper.
4. Grease silicone muffin cups with a bit of olive oil.
5. Divide the chickpea mixture evenly among 4 muffin cups.
6. Place the muffin cups in the air fryer basket and air fry at 190°C for 12-15 minutes or until the frittatas are set and golden brown.
7. Once cooked, remove from the air fryer, let them cool slightly, and garnish with chopped fresh parsley before serving.

CHAPTER 4
Main Recipes

Air-Fried Chicken Tikka Masala Skewers

Serves: 4
Prep time: 20 minutes
Cook time: 15 minutes

Ingredients:
- 500g boneless, skinless chicken thighs, cut into chunks
- 150g plain Greek yoghurt
- 2 tbsp tomato paste
- 1 tbsp garam masala
- 1 tbsp ground cumin
- 1 tbsp ground coriander
- 1 tsp smoked paprika
- 2 cloves garlic, minced
- 1-inch ginger, grated
- Juice of 1 lemon
- Salt and black pepper, to taste
- Fresh coriander, chopped, for garnish

Preparation instructions:
1. Preheat the Ninja Dual Zone Air Fryer to 200°C for 5 minutes.
2. In a bowl, mix together Greek yoghurt, tomato paste, garam masala, ground cumin, ground coriander, smoked paprika, minced garlic, grated ginger, lemon juice, salt, and black pepper.
3. Add the chicken chunks to the marinade, ensuring they are well-coated.
4. Thread the marinated chicken onto skewers.
5. Place the chicken skewers in the air fryer basket and air fry at 200°C for 12-15 minutes or until the chicken is cooked through, turning halfway.
6. Once done, remove from the air fryer, garnish with chopped fresh coriander, and serve.

Lemon Herb Tinned Salmon Parcels with Veggies

Serves: 4
Prep time: 15 minutes
Cook time: 15 minutes

Ingredients:
- 4 tinned salmon fillets, drained
- 200g baby potatoes, halved
- 150g broccoli florets
- 1 lemon, thinly sliced
- 2 tbsp olive oil
- 1 tsp dried dill
- 1 tsp dried parsley
- Salt and black pepper, to taste

Preparation instructions:
1. Preheat the Ninja Dual Zone Air Fryer to 190°C for 5 minutes.
2. In a bowl, toss halved baby potatoes and broccoli florets with olive oil, dried dill, dried parsley, salt, and black pepper.
3. Place each salmon fillet on a piece of foil or parchment paper.
4. Distribute the seasoned vegetables around each salmon fillet.
5. Top each salmon fillet with a couple of lemon slices.
6. Fold the foil or parchment paper to create parcels, ensuring they are sealed.
7. Place the salmon parcels in the air fryer basket and air fry at 190°C for 12-15 minutes or until the vegetables are tender and the salmon is cooked.
8. Once done, remove from the air fryer, carefully open the parcels, and serve.

BBQ Pulled Pork Stuffed Sweet Potatoes

Serves: 4
Prep time: 10 minutes
Cook time: 30 minutes

Ingredients:
- 500g cooked pulled pork
- 4 medium-sized sweet potatoes
- 120ml BBQ sauce
- 60g shredded cheddar cheese
- Fresh chives, chopped, for garnish
- Salt and black pepper, to taste

Preparation instructions:
1. Preheat the Ninja Dual Zone Air Fryer to 200°C for 5 minutes.
2. Microwave or bake sweet potatoes until tender.
3. Cut a slit lengthwise in each sweet potato, creating a pocket for the filling.
4. In a bowl, mix pulled pork with BBQ sauce, salt, and black pepper.
5. Stuff each sweet potato with the BBQ pulled pork mixture.
6. Place the stuffed sweet potatoes in the air fryer basket and air fry at 200°C for 10-12 minutes or until heated through.
7. In the last few minutes, sprinkle shredded cheddar cheese on top of each stuffed sweet potato until melted.
8. Once done, remove from the air fryer, garnish with chopped fresh chives, and serve.

Spinach and Ricotta-Stuffed Chicken Breasts

Serves: 4
Prep time: 15 minutes
Cook time: 25 minutes

Ingredients:
- 4 boneless, skinless chicken breasts
- 200g fresh spinach, chopped
- 150g ricotta cheese
- 1 clove garlic, minced
- 1 tbsp olive oil
- Salt and black pepper, to taste
- 1 lemon, sliced (for garnish)
- Fresh parsley, chopped (for garnish)

Preparation instructions:
1. Preheat the Ninja Dual Zone Air Fryer to 200°C for 5 minutes.
2. In a pan, sauté chopped spinach with olive oil and minced garlic until wilted. Allow it to cool.
3. In a bowl, mix the sautéed spinach with ricotta cheese, salt, and black pepper.
4. Cut a pocket into each chicken breast and stuff it with the spinach and ricotta mixture.
5. Place the stuffed chicken breasts in the air fryer basket.
6. Air fry at 200°C for 20-25 minutes or until the chicken is cooked through and the exterior is golden brown.
7. Garnish with sliced lemon and chopped fresh parsley before serving.

Vegan Chickpea and Vegetable Kebabs

Serves: 4
Prep time: 20 minutes
Cook time: 15 minutes

Ingredients:
- 400g canned chickpeas, drained and rinsed
- 1 red pepper, diced
- 1 courgette, diced
- 1 red onion, diced
- 2 tbsp olive oil
- 1 tsp ground cumin
- 1 tsp smoked paprika
- 1/2 tsp garlic powder
- Salt and black pepper, to taste
- Wooden skewers, soaked in water

Preparation instructions:
1. Preheat the Ninja Dual Zone Air Fryer to 190°C for 5 minutes.
2. In a bowl, toss chickpeas, diced red pepper, diced courgette, and diced red onion with olive oil, ground cumin, smoked paprika, garlic powder, salt, and black pepper.
3. Thread the marinated chickpeas and vegetables onto wooden skewers.
4. Place the kebabs in the air fryer basket.
5. Air fry at 190°C for 12-15 minutes or until the vegetables are tender and slightly charred.
6. Once done, remove from the air fryer and serve the Vegan Chickpea and Vegetable Kebabs.

Pesto Crusted Cod with Roasted Vegetables

Serves: 4
Prep time: 15 minutes
Cook time: 20 minutes

Ingredients:
- 4 cod fillets
- 4 tbsp basil pesto
- 500g mixed vegetables (e.g., cherry tomatoes, bell peppers, baby potatoes)
- 2 tbsp olive oil
- Salt and black pepper, to taste
- Fresh basil, chopped (for garnish)

Preparation instructions:
1. Preheat the Ninja Dual Zone Air Fryer to 200°C for 5 minutes.
2. Coat each cod fillet with a tablespoon of basil pesto.
3. In a bowl, toss mixed vegetables with olive oil, salt, and black pepper.
4. Place the pesto-coated cod fillets and the mixed vegetables in the air fryer basket.
5. Air fry at 200°C for 18-20 minutes or until the cod is cooked and the vegetables are roasted.
6. Once done, remove from the air fryer and garnish with chopped fresh basil before serving.

Thai-Inspired Basil Chicken Stir-Fry

Serves: 4
Prep time: 15 minutes
Cook time: 10 minutes

Ingredients:
- 500g boneless, skinless chicken breasts, thinly sliced
- 2 tbsp soy sauce
- 1 tbsp oyster sauce
- 1 tbsp fish sauce
- 1 tbsp sugar
- 2 tbsp vegetable oil
- 3 cloves garlic, minced
- 1 red chilli, sliced
- 1 pepper, thinly sliced
- 1 onion, thinly sliced
- 100g fresh basil leaves
- Cooked jasmine rice, for serving

Preparation instructions:
1. Preheat the Ninja Dual Zone Air Fryer to 200°C for 5 minutes.
2. In a bowl, mix sliced chicken with soy sauce, oyster sauce, fish sauce, and sugar. Let it marinate for 10 minutes.
3. Heat vegetable oil in a pan over medium heat. Add minced garlic and sliced red chilli, sauté until fragrant.
4. Add marinated chicken to the pan and stir-fry until cooked through.
5. Add sliced pepper and onion to the pan, continue to stir-fry until vegetables are tender.
6. Stir in fresh basil leaves until wilted.
7. Serve the Thai-Inspired Basil Chicken over cooked jasmine rice.

Air-Fried Mushroom and Lentil Burgers

Makes: 4 patties
Prep time: 20 minutes
Cook time: 15 minutes

Ingredients:
- 200g button mushrooms, finely chopped
- 200g cooked green lentils, mashed
- 1 onion, finely chopped
- 2 cloves garlic, minced
- 1 tsp cumin
- 1 tsp smoked paprika
- Salt and black pepper, to taste
- 2 tbsp olive oil
- 4 whole wheat burger buns
- Lettuce, tomato, and other desired toppings

Preparation instructions:
1. Preheat the Ninja Dual Zone Air Fryer to 180°C for 5 minutes.
2. In a pan, sauté chopped mushrooms, chopped onion, and minced garlic in olive oil until softened.
3. In a bowl, mix the sautéed mushrooms and onions with mashed lentils, cumin, smoked paprika, salt, and black pepper.
4. Form the mixture into four burger patties.
5. Place the patties in the air fryer basket and air fry at 180°C for 12-15 minutes or until golden brown and cooked through.
6. Serve the Mushroom and Lentil Burgers on whole wheat buns with desired toppings.

Teriyaki Glazed Tofu with Sesame Broccoli

Serves: 4
Prep time: 15 minutes
Cook time: 15 minutes

Ingredients:
- 400g firm tofu, cubed
- 2 tbsp soy sauce
- 1 tbsp rice vinegar
- 1 tbsp honey
- 1 tbsp sesame oil
- 500g broccoli, cut into florets
- 1 tbsp sesame seeds, toasted
- Spring onions, sliced, for garnish
- Cooked brown rice, for serving
- 4 tbsp teriyaki sauce

Preparation instructions:
1. Preheat the Ninja Dual Zone Air Fryer to 200°C for 5 minutes.
2. In a bowl, toss tofu cubes with teriyaki sauce, soy sauce, rice vinegar, honey, and sesame oil.
3. Place marinated tofu in the air fryer basket and air fry at 200°C for 15 minutes or until crispy.
4. In the last 5 minutes of cooking, add broccoli florets to the air fryer basket and continue cooking until tender-crisp.
5. Sprinkle toasted sesame seeds over the tofu and broccoli.
6. Serve the Teriyaki Glazed Tofu and Sesame Broccoli over cooked brown rice, garnished with sliced spring onions.

Moroccan Spiced Lamb Meatballs

Serves: 4
Prep time: 20 minutes
Cook time: 15 minutes

Ingredients:
- 500g lamb mince
- 1 onion, finely chopped
- 2 cloves garlic, minced
- 2 tsp ground cumin
- 2 tsp ground coriander
- 1 tsp smoked paprika
- 1/2 tsp cinnamon
- 1/4 tsp cayenne pepper
- Salt and black pepper, to taste
- Fresh coriander, chopped, for garnish
- Lemon wedges, for serving

Preparation instructions:
1. Preheat the Ninja Dual Zone Air Fryer to 200°C for 5 minutes.
2. In a bowl, combine lamb mince, finely chopped onion, minced garlic, ground cumin, ground coriander, smoked paprika, cinnamon, cayenne pepper, salt, and black pepper.
3. Form the mixture into meatballs and place them in the air fryer basket.
4. Air fry at 200°C for 12-15 minutes or until the meatballs are cooked through and browned.
5. Garnish with chopped fresh coriander and serve with lemon wedges.

Crispy Coconut-Crusted Shrimp with Mango Salsa

Serves: 4
Prep time: 15 minutes
Cook time: 10 minutes

Ingredients:
- 400g large shrimp, peeled and deveined
- 100g desiccated coconut
- 50g breadcrumbs
- 2 eggs, beaten
- 1 tsp garlic powder
- 1 tsp onion powder
- Salt and black pepper, to taste
- Cooking spray
- Fresh oregano, chopped, for garnish

Mango Salsa:
- 1 ripe mango, diced
- 1/2 red onion, finely chopped
- 1 small red chilli, minced
- Juice of 1 lime
- Salt, to taste

Preparation instructions:
1. Preheat the Ninja Dual Zone Air Fryer to 200°C for 5 minutes.
2. In one bowl, mix desiccated coconut, breadcrumbs, garlic powder, onion powder, salt, and black pepper.
3. Dip each shrimp into beaten eggs and then coat with the coconut mixture.
4. Place the coated shrimp in the air fryer basket, ensuring they are not touching.
5. Air fry at 200°C for 8-10 minutes or until the shrimp are golden and crispy.
6. In a separate bowl, combine diced mango, finely chopped red onion, minced red chilli, lime juice, and salt to make the salsa.
7. Serve the Crispy Coconut-Crusted Shrimp with Mango Salsa, garnished with chopped fresh oregano.

Ratatouille-Stuffed Peppers

Serves: 4
Prep time: 25 minutes
Cook time: 20 minutes

Ingredients:
- 2 large peppers, halved and seeds removed
- 1 courgette, diced
- 1 aubergine, diced
- 2 tomatoes, diced
- 1 onion, finely chopped
- 2 cloves garlic, minced
- 2 tbsp olive oil
- 1 tsp dried thyme
- 1 tsp dried oregano
- Salt and black pepper, to taste
- Fresh basil, chopped, for garnish

Preparation instructions:
1. Preheat the Ninja Dual Zone Air Fryer to 190°C for 5 minutes.
2. In a pan, sauté diced courgette, diced aubergine, diced tomatoes, finely chopped onion, and minced garlic in olive oil until softened.
3. Stir in dried thyme, dried oregano, salt, and black pepper.
4. Fill each halved pepper with the ratatouille mixture.
5. Place the stuffed peppers in the air fryer basket.
6. Air fry at 190°C for 18-20 minutes or until the peppers are tender.
7. Garnish with chopped fresh basil before serving.

Crusted Mustard Pork Chops with Apple Compote

Serves: 4
Prep time: 15 minutes
Cook time: 20 minutes

Ingredients:
- 4 pork chops
- 100g breadcrumbs
- 1 tsp dried thyme

Apple Compote:
- 2 apples, peeled, cored, and diced
- 2 tbsp brown sugar
- 60ml apple juice
- 2 tbsp Dijon mustard
- 50g grated Parmesan cheese
- Salt and black pepper, to taste
- 2 tbsp unsalted butter
- 1/2 tsp cinnamon

Preparation instructions:
1. Preheat the Ninja Dual Zone Air Fryer to 200°C for 5 minutes.
2. In a bowl, mix Dijon mustard, breadcrumbs, grated Parmesan, dried thyme, salt, and black pepper.
3. Coat each pork chop with the mustard mixture, pressing it on both sides.
4. Place the crusted pork chops in the air fryer basket.
5. Air fry at 200°C for 18-20 minutes or until the pork is cooked and the crust is golden brown.
6. In a saucepan, combine diced apples, unsalted butter, brown sugar, cinnamon, and apple juice. Cook until the apples are soft and the mixture thickens.
7. Serve the Crusted Mustard Pork Chops with a spoonful of Apple Compote.

Spinach and Feta Stuffed Portobello Mushrooms

Serves: 4
Prep time: 15 minutes
Cook time: 12 minutes

Ingredients:
- 4 large Portobello mushrooms
- 200g fresh spinach, chopped
- 150g feta cheese, crumbled
- 2 cloves garlic, minced
- 2 tbsp olive oil
- Salt and black pepper, to taste

Preparation instructions:
1. Preheat the Ninja Dual Zone Air Fryer to 190°C for 5 minutes.
2. Remove the stems from the Portobello mushrooms and brush the caps with olive oil.
3. In a pan, sauté chopped spinach and minced garlic in olive oil until wilted. Season with salt and black pepper.
4. Fill each mushroom cap with the sautéed spinach and top with crumbled feta.
5. Place the stuffed mushrooms in the air fryer basket.
6. Air fry at 190°C for 10-12 minutes or until the mushrooms are tender and the feta is lightly browned.

Air-Fried Vegetable Paella with Saffron Rice

Serves: 4
Prep time: 20 minutes
Cook time: 25 minutes

Ingredients:
- 300g paella rice
- 1 onion, finely chopped
- 2 cloves garlic, minced
- 1 red pepper, diced
- 1 yellow pepper, diced
- 150g green beans, trimmed and halved
- 1 tsp saffron threads, soaked in 60ml hot water
- 800ml vegetable broth
- 1 tsp smoked paprika
- Salt and black pepper, to taste
- Lemon wedges, for serving

Preparation instructions:
1. Preheat the Ninja Dual Zone Air Fryer to 200°C for 5 minutes.
2. In a pan, sauté chopped onion and minced garlic until translucent.
3. Add diced red and yellow peppers, green beans, and sauté for an additional 5 minutes.
4. Stir in paella rice, soaked saffron threads with water, smoked paprika, salt, and black pepper.
5. Transfer the rice mixture to the air fryer basket.
6. Pour vegetable broth over the rice mixture.
7. Air fry at 200°C for 25 minutes or until the rice is cooked and forms a crispy bottom.
8. Serve the Air-Fried Vegetable Paella with lemon wedges on the side.

CHAPTER 5
Fish and Seafood

Garlic Butter Lemon and Herb Shrimp Skewers

Serves: 4
Prep time: 15 minutes
Cook time: 10 minutes

Ingredients:
- 400g large shrimp, peeled and deveined
- 3 tbsp unsalted butter, melted
- 2 cloves garlic, minced
- Zest of 1 lemon
- 1 tbsp fresh parsley, chopped
- 1 tsp dried oregano
- Salt and black pepper, to taste
- Lemon wedges, for serving

Preparation instructions:
1. Preheat the Ninja Dual Zone Air Fryer to 200°C for 5 minutes.
2. In a bowl, combine melted butter, minced garlic, lemon zest, chopped fresh parsley, dried oregano, salt, and black pepper.
3. Thread the shrimp on skewers.
4. Brush the shrimp skewers with the garlic butter mixture.
5. Place the skewers in the air fryer basket.
6. Air fry at 200°C for 8-10 minutes or until the shrimp are opaque and cooked through.
7. Serve the Garlic Butter Lemon and Herb Shrimp Skewers with lemon wedges on the side.

Cajun-Style Air-Fried Haddock Nuggets

Serves: 4
Prep time: 20 minutes
Cook time: 15 minutes

Ingredients:
- 400g haddock fillets, cut into bite-sized nuggets
- 2 tbsp olive oil
- 2 tsp Cajun seasoning
- 1 tsp garlic powder
- 1 tsp onion powder
- 1/2 tsp smoked paprika
- 1/4 tsp cayenne pepper
- 100g breadcrumbs
- Salt and black pepper, to taste
- Lemon wedges, for serving

Preparation instructions:
1. Preheat the Ninja Dual Zone Air Fryer to 190°C for 5 minutes.
2. In a bowl, toss haddock nuggets with olive oil, Cajun seasoning, garlic powder, onion powder, smoked paprika, cayenne pepper, salt, and black pepper.
3. Coat each nugget with breadcrumbs.
4. Place the coated haddock nuggets in the air fryer basket.
5. Air fry at 190°C for 12-15 minutes or until the nuggets are golden brown and cooked through.
6. Serve the Cajun-Style Air-Fried Haddock Nuggets with lemon wedges.

Coconut-Crusted Haddock Bites with Pineapple Salsa

Serves: 4
Prep time: 25 minutes
Cook time: 15 minutes

Ingredients:
- 400g haddock fillets, cut into bite-sized pieces
- 100g shredded coconut
- 50g panko breadcrumbs
- 2 eggs, beaten
- 1 tsp garlic powder
- 1 tsp onion powder
- Salt and black pepper, to taste

Pineapple Salsa:
- 200g fresh pineapple, diced
- 1/2 red onion, finely chopped
- 1 red chilli, minced
- 2 tbsp fresh coriander, chopped
- Juice of 1 lime
- Salt, to taste

Preparation instructions:
1. Preheat the Ninja Dual Zone Air Fryer to 200°C for 5 minutes.
2. In a bowl, mix shredded coconut, panko breadcrumbs, garlic powder, onion powder, salt, and black pepper.
3. Dip each haddock piece into beaten eggs and then coat with the coconut mixture.
4. Place the coated haddock bites in the air fryer basket.
5. Air fry at 200°C for 12-15 minutes or until the bites are crispy and golden.
6. In a separate bowl, combine diced pineapple, finely chopped red onion, minced red chilli, chopped fresh coriander, lime juice, and salt to make the salsa.
7. Serve the Coconut-Crusted Haddock Bites with Pineapple Salsa on the side.

Mediterranean Stuffed Calamari Rings

Serves: 4
Prep time: 20 minutes
Cook time: 15 minutes

Ingredients:
- 400g calamari rings
- 200g cherry tomatoes, diced
- 100g feta cheese, crumbled
- 1/2 red onion, finely chopped
- 2 tbsp fresh parsley, chopped
- 2 tbsp olive oil
- 1 lemon, juiced
- 1 tsp dried oregano
- Salt and black pepper, to taste

Preparation instructions:
1. Preheat the Ninja Dual Zone Air Fryer to 200°C for 5 minutes.
2. In a bowl, combine diced cherry tomatoes, crumbled feta, finely chopped red onion, chopped fresh parsley, olive oil, lemon juice, dried oregano, salt, and black pepper.
3. Stuff each calamari ring with the Mediterranean mixture.
4. Place the stuffed calamari rings in the air fryer basket.
5. Air fry at 200°C for 12-15 minutes or until the calamari is cooked and slightly golden.
6. Serve the Mediterranean Stuffed Calamari Rings with additional lemon wedges.

Smoked Paprika Prawn Tacos

Serves: 4
Prep time: 15 minutes
Cook time: 8 minutes

Ingredients:
- 400g large prawns, peeled and deveined
- 2 tbsp olive oil
- 1 tsp smoked paprika
- 1/2 tsp garlic powder
- 1/2 tsp onion powder
- 1/2 tsp cumin
- 1/4 tsp cayenne pepper
- Salt and black pepper, to taste
- 8 small corn tortillas
- 100g shredded lettuce
- 1 avocado, sliced
- 1 lime, cut into wedges

Preparation instructions:
1. Preheat the Ninja Dual Zone Air Fryer to 200°C for 5 minutes.
2. In a bowl, toss prawns with olive oil, smoked paprika, garlic powder, onion powder, cumin, cayenne pepper, salt, and black pepper.
3. Place the seasoned prawns in the air fryer basket.
4. Air fry at 200°C for 8 minutes or until the prawns are cooked and slightly charred.
5. Warm the corn tortillas in the air fryer for 1-2 minutes.
6. Assemble the tacos with shredded lettuce, sliced avocado, and smoked paprika prawns.
7. Serve the Smoked Paprika Prawn Tacos with lime wedges.

Crispy Tilapia with Dill Yoghurt Sauce

Serves: 4
Prep time: 15 minutes
Cook time: 12 minutes

Ingredients:
- 4 tilapia fillets
- 100g breadcrumbs
- 2 tbsp grated Parmesan cheese
- 1 tsp dried dill
- 1/2 tsp garlic powder
- 1/2 tsp onion powder
- 1/4 tsp paprika
- Salt and black pepper, to taste

Dill Yoghurt Sauce:
- 150g Greek yoghurt
- 1 tbsp fresh dill, chopped
- 1 tbsp lemon juice
- Salt and black pepper, to taste

Preparation instructions:
1. Preheat the Ninja Dual Zone Air Fryer to 200°C for 5 minutes.
2. In a bowl, mix breadcrumbs, grated Parmesan, dried dill, garlic powder, onion powder, paprika, salt, and black pepper.
3. Coat each tilapia fillet with the breadcrumb mixture.
4. Place the coated tilapia fillets in the air fryer basket.
5. Air fry at 200°C for 10-12 minutes or until the tilapia is crispy and cooked through.
6. In a small bowl, combine Greek yoghurt, chopped fresh dill, lemon juice, salt, and black pepper to make the dill yoghurt sauce.
7. Serve the Crispy Tilapia with a dollop of Dill Yoghurt Sauce on the side.

Lemon Pepper Cod Bites

Serves: 4
Prep time: 15 minutes
Cook time: 10 minutes

Ingredients:
- 400g cod fillets, cut into bite-sized pieces
- 50g breadcrumbs
- 1 tsp lemon zest
- 1/2 tsp black pepper
- 1/4 tsp garlic powder
- 1/4 tsp onion powder
- 1/4 tsp paprika
- 2 tbsp olive oil
- Lemon wedges, for serving

Preparation instructions:
1. Preheat the Ninja Dual Zone Air Fryer to 200°C for 5 minutes.
2. In a bowl, mix breadcrumbs, lemon zest, black pepper, garlic powder, onion powder, and paprika.
3. Toss cod bites in olive oil, then coat with the breadcrumb mixture.
4. Place the coated cod bites in the air fryer basket.
5. Air fry at 200°C for 8-10 minutes or until the cod is crispy and cooked through.
6. Serve the Lemon Pepper Cod Bites with lemon wedges on the side.

Herbed Breadcrumb-Crusted Cod Fillets

Serves: 4
Prep time: 20 minutes
Cook time: 12 minutes

Ingredients:
- 4 cod fillets
- 100g breadcrumbs
- 2 tbsp fresh parsley, chopped
- 1 tbsp fresh dill, chopped
- 1 tsp lemon zest
- 1/2 tsp garlic powder
- 1/2 tsp onion powder
- Salt and black pepper, to taste
- 2 tbsp olive oil

Preparation instructions:
1. Preheat the Ninja Dual Zone Air Fryer to 190°C for 5 minutes.
2. In a bowl, mix breadcrumbs, chopped fresh parsley, chopped fresh dill, lemon zest, garlic powder, onion powder, salt, and black pepper.
3. Brush each cod fillet with olive oil, then coat with the breadcrumb mixture.
4. Place the coated cod fillets in the air fryer basket.
5. Air fry at 190°C for 10-12 minutes or until the cod is golden brown and flakes easily.
6. Serve the Herbed Breadcrumb-Crusted Cod Fillets with a sprinkle of fresh herbs.

Chilli Lime Grilled Salmon Patties

Serves: 4
Prep time: 25 minutes
Cook time: 15 minutes

Ingredients:
- 400g salmon fillets, skinless and boneless
- 1 red chilli, finely chopped
- Zest of 1 lime
- 2 tbsp fresh coriander, chopped
- 1 tsp ground cumin
- 1/2 tsp garlic powder
- 1/2 tsp onion powder
- Salt and black pepper, to taste
- 2 tbsp olive oil

Preparation instructions:
1. Preheat the Ninja Dual Zone Air Fryer to 200°C for 5 minutes.
2. In a food processor, pulse salmon until coarsely ground.
3. In a bowl, combine ground salmon, chopped red chilli, lime zest, chopped fresh coriander, ground cumin, garlic powder, onion powder, salt, and black pepper.
4. Shape the mixture into salmon patties.
5. Brush each patty with olive oil.
6. Place the salmon patties in the air fryer basket.
7. Air fry at 200°C for 12-15 minutes or until the patties are cooked through and golden.
8. Serve the Chilli Lime Grilled Salmon Patties with additional lime wedges.

Thai Red Curry Mussels in the Air Fryer

Serves: 4
Prep time: 15 minutes
Cook time: 8 minutes

Ingredients:
- 800g fresh mussels, cleaned and debearded
- 200ml coconut milk
- 2 tbsp Thai red curry paste
- 1 tbsp fish sauce
- 1 tbsp brown sugar
- 1 red chilli, sliced
- 2 spring onions, chopped
- Fresh coriander, for garnish
- Lime wedges, for serving

Preparation instructions:
1. Preheat the Ninja Dual Zone Air Fryer to 200°C for 5 minutes.
2. In a bowl, mix coconut milk, Thai red curry paste, fish sauce, and brown sugar.
3. Place cleaned mussels in the air fryer basket.
4. Pour the curry mixture over the mussels.
5. Air fry at 200°C for 8 minutes or until the mussels are fully cooked.
6. Garnish with sliced red chilli, chopped spring onions, and fresh coriander.
7. Serve the Thai Red Curry Mussels with lime wedges.

Zesty Tandoori Grilled Tuna Steaks

Serves: 4
Prep time: 20 minutes
Cook time: 10 minutes

Ingredients:
- 4 tuna steaks (150g each)
- 100g Greek yoghurt
- 2 tbsp tandoori paste
- 1 tbsp lemon juice
- 1 tsp ground cumin
- 1 tsp ground coriander
- 1/2 tsp paprika
- Salt and black pepper, to taste
- Fresh mint, for garnish

Preparation instructions:
1. Preheat the Ninja Dual Zone Air Fryer to 200°C for 5 minutes.
2. In a bowl, mix Greek yoghurt, tandoori paste, lemon juice, ground cumin, ground coriander, paprika, salt, and black pepper.
3. Coat each tuna steak with the tandoori marinade.
4. Place the marinated tuna steaks in the air fryer basket.
5. Air fry at 200°C for 10 minutes or until the tuna is cooked to your liking.
6. Garnish with fresh mint before serving.

Spicy Harissa Marinated Grilled Shrimp

Serves: 4
Prep time: 15 minutes
Cook time: 6 minutes

Ingredients:
- 400g large shrimp, peeled and deveined
- 2 tbsp harissa paste
- 2 tbsp olive oil
- 1 tsp ground cumin
- 1 tsp ground coriander
- 1/2 tsp smoked paprika
- 1/4 tsp cayenne pepper
- Salt and black pepper, to taste
- Lemon wedges, for serving

Preparation instructions:
1. Preheat the Ninja Dual Zone Air Fryer to 200°C for 5 minutes.
2. In a bowl, mix harissa paste, olive oil, ground cumin, ground coriander, smoked paprika, cayenne pepper, salt, and black pepper.
3. Toss shrimp in the harissa marinade until well-coated.
4. Place the marinated shrimp in the air fryer basket.
5. Air fry at 200°C for 6 minutes or until the shrimp are cooked through.
6. Serve the Spicy Harissa Marinated Grilled Shrimp with lemon wedges.

Sesame Crusted Tuna Steaks with Wasabi Mayo

Serves: 4
Prep time: 15 minutes
Cook time: 8 minutes

Ingredients:
- 4 tuna steaks (150g each)
- 50g sesame seeds
- 1 tbsp soy sauce
- 1 tbsp sesame oil
- 1 tsp honey
- 1/2 tsp ground ginger
- Salt and black pepper, to taste

Preparation instructions:
1. Preheat the Ninja Dual Zone Air Fryer to 200°C for 5 minutes.
2. In a bowl, mix sesame seeds, soy sauce, sesame oil, honey, ground ginger, salt, and black pepper.
3. Coat each tuna steak with the sesame seed mixture.
4. Place the coated tuna steaks in the air fryer basket.
5. Air fry at 200°C for 8 minutes or until the tuna is seared on the outside and pink in the middle.
6. Serve the Sesame Crusted Tuna Steaks with Wasabi Mayo.

Teriyaki Glazed Salmon Skewers with Bok Choy

Serves: 4
Prep time: 20 minutes
Cook time: 10 minutes

Ingredients:
- 400g salmon fillets, cut into chunks
- 4 bok choy, halved
- 60ml teriyaki sauce
- 2 tbsp olive oil
- 1 tbsp rice vinegar
- 1 tsp garlic powder
- 1/2 tsp ground black pepper

Preparation instructions:
1. Preheat the Ninja Dual Zone Air Fryer to 200°C for 5 minutes.
2. In a bowl, mix teriyaki sauce, olive oil, rice vinegar, garlic powder, and ground black pepper.
3. Thread salmon chunks and bok choy onto skewers.
4. Brush the skewers with the teriyaki mixture.
5. Place the skewers in the air fryer basket.
6. Air fry at 200°C for 10 minutes or until the salmon is cooked through.
7. Serve the Teriyaki Glazed Salmon Skewers with Bok Choy.

Moroccan Spiced Sea Bass Parcels

Serves: 4
Prep time: 25 minutes
Cook time: 12 minutes

Ingredients:
- 4 sea bass fillets
- 2 tbsp olive oil
- 1 tbsp ground cumin
- 1 tbsp ground coriander
- 1 tsp smoked paprika
- 1/2 tsp ground cinnamon
- 1/4 tsp cayenne pepper
- Salt and black pepper, to taste
- Fresh lemon wedges, for serving

Preparation instructions:
1. Preheat the Ninja Dual Zone Air Fryer to 190°C for 5 minutes.
2. In a bowl, mix olive oil, ground cumin, ground coriander, smoked paprika, ground cinnamon, cayenne pepper, salt, and black pepper.
3. Coat each sea bass fillet with the spice mixture.
4. Place each fillet in an individual foil parcel.
5. Put the foil parcels in the air fryer basket.
6. Air fry at 190°C for 12 minutes or until the sea bass is flaky.
7. Serve the Moroccan Spiced Sea Bass Parcels with fresh lemon wedges.

CHAPTER 6
Poultry and Meat Recipes

Rosemary and Garlic Air-Fried Lamb Chops

Serves: 4
Prep time: 15 minutes
Cook time: 12 minutes

Ingredients:
- 4 lamb chops
- 2 tbsp olive oil
- 2 cloves garlic, minced
- 1 tbsp fresh rosemary, chopped
- Salt and black pepper, to taste
- Lemon wedges, for serving

Preparation instructions:
1. Preheat the Ninja Dual Zone Air Fryer to 200°C for 5 minutes.
2. In a bowl, mix olive oil, minced garlic, chopped rosemary, salt, and black pepper.
3. Coat each lamb chop with the rosemary and garlic mixture.
4. Place the lamb chops in the air fryer basket.
5. Air fry at 200°C for 12 minutes or until the lamb is cooked to your liking.
6. Serve the Rosemary and Garlic Air-Fried Lamb Chops with lemon wedges.

Sticky Honey Mustard Chicken Drumsticks

Serves: 4
Prep time: 20 minutes
Cook time: 15 minutes

Ingredients:
- 8 chicken drumsticks
- 60ml honey
- 2 tbsp Dijon mustard
- 1 tbsp soy sauce
- 1 tbsp olive oil
- 1 tsp garlic powder
- Salt and black pepper, to taste
- Sesame seeds, for garnish

Preparation instructions:
1. Preheat the Ninja Dual Zone Air Fryer to 180°C for 5 minutes.
2. In a bowl, mix honey, Dijon mustard, soy sauce, olive oil, garlic powder, salt, and black pepper.
3. Coat each chicken drumstick with the honey mustard mixture.
4. Place the drumsticks in the air fryer basket.
5. Air fry at 180°C for 15 minutes or until the chicken is cooked through.
6. Garnish the Sticky Honey Mustard Chicken Drumsticks with sesame seeds before serving.

Paprika-Rubbed Air-Fried Pork Tenderloin

Serves: 4
Prep time: 15 minutes
Cook time: 20 minutes

Ingredients:
- 500g pork tenderloin
- 2 tbsp olive oil
- 1 tbsp smoked paprika
- 1 tsp garlic powder
- 1 tsp onion powder
- 1/2 tsp dried thyme
- Salt and black pepper, to taste

Preparation instructions:
1. Preheat the Ninja Dual Zone Air Fryer to 200°C for 5 minutes.
2. In a bowl, mix olive oil, smoked paprika, garlic powder, onion powder, dried thyme, salt, and black pepper.
3. Coat the pork tenderloin with the paprika rub.
4. Place the pork tenderloin in the air fryer basket.
5. Air fry at 200°C for 20 minutes or until the pork is cooked and reaches the desired internal temperature.
6. Let the Paprika-Rubbed Air-Fried Pork Tenderloin rest before slicing and serving.

Spiced Apricot Glazed Chicken Breast

Serves: 4
Prep time: 15 minutes
Cook time: 20 minutes

Ingredients:
- 4 chicken breasts
- 80g apricot jam
- 1 tbsp olive oil
- 1 tsp ground cumin
- 1 tsp smoked paprika
- 1/2 tsp cayenne pepper
- Salt and black pepper, to taste
- Fresh parsley, for garnish

Preparation instructions:
1. Preheat the Ninja Dual Zone Air Fryer to 200°C for 5 minutes.
2. In a bowl, mix apricot jam, olive oil, ground cumin, smoked paprika, cayenne pepper, salt, and black pepper.
3. Coat each chicken breast with the spiced apricot glaze.
4. Place the chicken breasts in the air fryer basket.
5. Air fry at 200°C for 20 minutes or until the chicken is cooked through.
6. Garnish the Spiced Apricot Glazed Chicken Breast with fresh parsley before serving.

Jerk Chicken Thighs with Mango Salsa

Serves: 4
Prep time: 20 minutes
Cook time: 18 minutes

Ingredients:
- 8 chicken thighs
- 2 tbsp jerk seasoning
- 1 tbsp olive oil
- 2 mangoes, diced
- 1 red onion, finely chopped
- 1 red chilli, finely chopped
- Juice of 1 lime
- Fresh coriander, for garnish
- Salt, to taste

Preparation instructions:
1. Preheat the Ninja Dual Zone Air Fryer to 190°C for 5 minutes.
2. In a bowl, toss chicken thighs with jerk seasoning and olive oil.
3. Place the seasoned chicken thighs in the air fryer basket.
4. Air fry at 190°C for 18 minutes or until the chicken is crispy and fully cooked.
5. In a separate bowl, mix diced mangoes, red onion, red chilli, lime juice, and salt to make the mango salsa.
6. Serve the Jerk Chicken Thighs with Mango Salsa, garnished with fresh coriander.

Maple Dijon Glazed Turkey Meatballs

Serves: 4
Prep time: 15 minutes
Cook time: 15 minutes

Ingredients:
- 500g ground turkey
- 60ml maple syrup
- 2 tbsp Dijon mustard
- 1 tbsp soy sauce
- 1 tbsp olive oil
- 2 cloves garlic, minced
- 1/2 tsp dried thyme
- Salt and black pepper, to taste
- Sesame seeds, for garnish

Preparation instructions:
1. Preheat the Ninja Dual Zone Air Fryer to 180°C for 5 minutes.
2. In a bowl, mix ground turkey, maple syrup, Dijon mustard, soy sauce, olive oil, minced garlic, dried thyme, salt, and black pepper.
3. Form the mixture into meatballs and place them in the air fryer basket.
4. Air fry at 180°C for 15 minutes or until the turkey meatballs are cooked through.
5. Garnish the Maple Dijon Glazed Turkey Meatballs with sesame seeds before serving.

Pesto Marinated Grilled Chicken Skewers

Serves: 4
Prep time: 15 minutes
Cook time: 15 minutes

Ingredients:
- 500g chicken breast, cut into cubes
- 60g pesto sauce
- 2 tbsp olive oil
- 1 lemon, juiced
- 2 cloves garlic, minced
- Salt and black pepper, to taste
- Fresh basil, for garnish

Preparation instructions:
1. Preheat the Ninja Dual Zone Air Fryer to 200°C for 5 minutes.
2. In a bowl, combine chicken cubes, pesto sauce, olive oil, lemon juice, minced garlic, salt, and black pepper.
3. Thread the marinated chicken onto skewers.
4. Place the chicken skewers in the air fryer basket.
5. Air fry at 200°C for 15 minutes or until the chicken is cooked through.
6. Garnish the Pesto Marinated Grilled Chicken Skewers with fresh basil before serving.

Mediterranean Lamb Kofta Patties

Serves: 4
Prep time: 20 minutes
Cook time: 12 minutes

Ingredients:
- 500g ground lamb
- 1/2 red onion, finely chopped
- 2 cloves garlic, minced
- 1 tsp ground cumin
- 1 tsp ground coriander
- 1/2 tsp smoked paprika
- Salt and black pepper, to taste
- 4 tbsp breadcrumbs
- 1 egg, beaten
- Fresh mint, for garnish

Preparation instructions:
1. Preheat the Ninja Dual Zone Air Fryer to 190°C for 5 minutes.
2. In a bowl, mix ground lamb, chopped red onion, minced garlic, ground cumin, ground coriander, smoked paprika, salt, black pepper, breadcrumbs, and beaten egg.
3. Form the mixture into patties and place them in the air fryer basket.
4. Air fry at 190°C for 12 minutes or until the lamb kofta patties are cooked through.
5. Garnish the Mediterranean Lamb Kofta Patties with fresh mint before serving.

Hoisin Ginger Glazed Pork Belly Slices

Serves: 4
Prep time: 15 minutes
Cook time: 20 minutes

Ingredients:
- 500g pork belly slices
- 4 tbsp hoisin sauce
- 2 tbsp soy sauce
- 1 tbsp honey
- 1 tbsp grated ginger
- 2 cloves garlic, minced
- Sesame seeds, for garnish
- Spring onions, sliced, for garnish

Preparation instructions:
1. Preheat the Ninja Dual Zone Air Fryer to 180°C for 5 minutes.
2. In a bowl, mix pork belly slices, hoisin sauce, soy sauce, honey, grated ginger, and minced garlic.
3. Place the marinated pork belly slices in the air fryer basket.
4. Air fry at 180°C for 20 minutes or until the pork belly slices are caramelised.
5. Garnish the Hoisin Ginger Glazed Pork Belly Slices with sesame seeds and sliced spring onions before serving.

Cranberry and Thyme Stuffed Chicken Thighs

Serves: 4
Prep time: 15 minutes
Cook time: 25 minutes

Ingredients:
- 500g chicken thighs, boneless and skinless
- 100g dried cranberries
- 2 tbsp fresh thyme, chopped
- 50g feta cheese, crumbled
- Salt and black pepper, to taste
- Olive oil, for brushing
- Fresh parsley, for garnish

Preparation instructions:
1. Preheat the Ninja Dual Zone Air Fryer to 180°C for 5 minutes.
2. In a bowl, mix dried cranberries, fresh thyme, crumbled feta, salt, and black pepper.
3. Make a pocket in each chicken thigh and stuff them with the cranberry and thyme mixture.
4. Brush the stuffed chicken thighs with olive oil.
5. Place the chicken thighs in the air fryer basket.
6. Air fry at 180°C for 25 minutes or until the chicken is cooked through.
7. Garnish the Cranberry and Thyme Stuffed Chicken Thighs with fresh parsley before serving.

Teriyaki Pineapple Turkey Burgers

Serves: 4
Prep time: 12 minutes
Cook time: 15 minutes

Ingredients:
- 500g ground turkey
- 100g pineapple, finely chopped
- 3 tbsp teriyaki sauce
- 2 tbsp breadcrumbs
- 1 tsp garlic powder
- Salt and black pepper, to taste
- 4 burger buns
- Lettuce, tomato, and red onion, for garnish

Preparation instructions:
1. Preheat the Ninja Dual Zone Air Fryer to 200°C for 5 minutes.
2. In a bowl, mix ground turkey, chopped pineapple, teriyaki sauce, breadcrumbs, garlic powder, salt, and black pepper.
3. Form the mixture into burger patties.
4. Place the turkey burgers in the air fryer basket.
5. Air fry at 200°C for 15 minutes or until the burgers are cooked through.
6. Serve the Teriyaki Pineapple Turkey Burgers on buns with lettuce, tomato, and red onion.

Cumin-Spiced Grilled Beef Kebabs

Serves: 4
Prep time: 20 minutes
Cook time: 15 minutes

Ingredients:
- 500g beef sirloin, cubed
- 2 tbsp olive oil
- 2 tsp ground cumin
- 1 tsp smoked paprika
- 1 tsp ground coriander
- Salt and black pepper, to taste
- Red and yellow peppers, onion, cherry tomatoes (for skewering)
- Fresh coriander, for garnish

Preparation instructions:
1. Preheat the Ninja Dual Zone Air Fryer to 200°C for 5 minutes.
2. In a bowl, mix beef cubes with olive oil, ground cumin, smoked paprika, ground coriander, salt, and black pepper.
3. Thread the marinated beef onto skewers with peppers, onion, and cherry tomatoes.
4. Place the beef kebabs in the air fryer basket.
5. Air fry at 200°C for 15 minutes or until the beef is grilled to perfection.
6. Garnish the Cumin-Spiced Grilled Beef Kebabs with fresh coriander before serving.

Herb-Crusted Pork Loin

Serves: 4
Prep time: 15 minutes
Cook time: 30 minutes

Ingredients:
- 500g pork loin, boneless
- 2 tbsp olive oil
- 2 tbsp fresh parsley, chopped
- 1 tbsp fresh thyme, chopped
- 1 tbsp fresh rosemary, chopped
- 2 cloves garlic, minced
- Salt and black pepper, to taste
- Lemon wedges, for serving

Preparation instructions:
1. Preheat the Ninja Dual Zone Air Fryer to 200°C for 5 minutes.
2. Rub the pork loin with olive oil, fresh parsley, fresh thyme, fresh rosemary, minced garlic, salt, and black pepper.
3. Place the herb-crusted pork loin in the air fryer basket.
4. Air fry at 200°C for 30 minutes or until the pork loin reaches a safe internal temperature.
5. Allow the pork loin to rest for a few minutes before slicing.
6. Serve with lemon wedges.

Lemon and Herb Butter Basted Chicken Thighs

Serves: 4
Prep time: 12 minutes
Cook time: 25 minutes

Ingredients:
- 600g chicken thighs, bone-in, skin-on
- 4 tbsp unsalted butter, melted
- Zest of 1 lemon
- 2 tbsp fresh parsley, chopped
- 1 tbsp fresh thyme, chopped
- Salt and black pepper, to taste

Preparation instructions:
1. Preheat the Ninja Dual Zone Air Fryer to 180°C for 5 minutes.
2. In a bowl, mix melted butter, lemon zest, fresh parsley, fresh thyme, salt, and black pepper.
3. Brush the chicken thighs with the lemon and herb butter mixture.
4. Place the chicken thighs in the air fryer basket.
5. Air fry at 180°C for 25 minutes or until the chicken is golden brown and cooked through.
6. Baste the chicken thighs with additional lemon and herb butter halfway through cooking.
7. Serve the Lemon and Herb Butter Basted Chicken Thighs hot.

Tandoori Spiced Chicken Wings

Serves: 4
Prep time: 10 minutes
Cook time: 20 minutes

Ingredients:
- 800g chicken wings
- 60ml plain yoghurt
- 2 tbsp tandoori spice mix
- 1 tbsp vegetable oil
- 1 tsp ground cumin
- 1 tsp ground coriander
- Salt and black pepper, to taste
- Fresh coriander, for garnish
- Lemon wedges, for serving

Preparation instructions:
1. Preheat the Ninja Dual Zone Air Fryer to 200°C for 5 minutes.
2. In a bowl, combine yoghurt, tandoori spice mix, vegetable oil, ground cumin, ground coriander, salt, and black pepper.
3. Coat the chicken wings with the tandoori marinade.
4. Place the marinated chicken wings in the air fryer basket.
5. Air fry at 200°C for 20 minutes or until the chicken wings are crispy and fully cooked.
6. Garnish with fresh coriander and serve with lemon wedges.

CHAPTER 7
Beans and Legumes

Spicy Chickpea and Spinach Air-Fried Patties

Serves: 4
Prep time: 15 minutes
Cook time: 20 minutes

Ingredients:
- 400g canned chickpeas, drained and rinsed
- 100g fresh spinach, finely chopped
- 50g breadcrumbs
- 1 small onion, finely chopped
- 2 cloves garlic, minced
- 1 tsp ground cumin
- 1 tsp ground coriander
- 1/2 tsp smoked paprika
- Salt and black pepper, to taste
- 2 tbsp olive oil
- Lemon wedges, for serving

Preparation instructions:
1. In a food processor, combine chickpeas, chopped spinach, breadcrumbs, chopped onion, minced garlic, ground cumin, ground coriander, smoked paprika, salt, and black pepper.
2. Pulse the mixture until well combined but still slightly chunky.
3. Shape the mixture into 8 patties.
4. Preheat the Ninja Dual Zone Air Fryer to 200°C for 5 minutes.
5. Brush the patties with olive oil.
6. Place the patties in the air fryer basket and air fry at 200°C for 20 minutes, turning halfway through, until they are golden brown and cooked through.
7. Serve the Spicy Chickpea and Spinach Air-Fried Patties with lemon wedges.

Curried Lentil and Sweet Potato Bites

Serves: 4
Prep time: 15 minutes
Cook time: 25 minutes

Ingredients:
- 200g red lentils, cooked
- 200g sweet potato, grated
- 1 small onion, finely chopped
- 2 cloves garlic, minced
- 1 tbsp curry powder
- 50g breadcrumbs
- Salt and black pepper, to taste
- 2 tbsp coconut oil
- Fresh coriander, for garnish
- Yoghurt for dipping

Preparation instructions:
1. In a bowl, combine cooked red lentils, grated sweet potato, chopped onion, minced garlic, curry powder, breadcrumbs, salt, and black pepper.
2. Shape the mixture into 12 bite-sized balls.
3. Preheat the Ninja Dual Zone Air Fryer to 190°C for 5 minutes.
4. Brush the lentil and sweet potato bites with coconut oil.
5. Place the bites in the air fryer basket and air fry at 190°C for 25 minutes, turning halfway through, until they are crispy and cooked through.
6. Garnish with fresh coriander and serve with yoghurt for dipping.

Air-Fried Black Bean and Corn Quesadillas

Serves: 4
Prep time: 12 minutes
Cook time: 15 minutes

Ingredients:
- 400g black beans, drained and rinsed
- 150g corn kernels
- 1 red pepper, diced
- 1 tsp ground cumin
- 1 tsp chilli powder
- Salt and black pepper, to taste
- 4 large whole wheat tortillas
- 200g shredded cheddar cheese
- Olive oil spray

Preparation instructions:
1. In a bowl, mix black beans, corn kernels, diced red pepper, ground cumin, chilli powder, salt, and black pepper.
2. Preheat the Ninja Dual Zone Air Fryer to 180°C for 5 minutes.
3. Place one tortilla on a flat surface and spread a quarter of the bean mixture on one half of the tortilla.
4. Sprinkle a quarter of the shredded cheddar cheese over the bean mixture.
5. Fold the tortilla in half, creating a quesadilla.
6. Repeat for the remaining tortillas.
7. Lightly spray both sides of each quesadilla with olive oil spray.
8. Place the quesadillas in the air fryer basket and air fry at 180°C for 15 minutes, turning halfway through, until they are golden brown and the cheese is melted.
9. Allow them to cool for a few minutes before slicing and serving.

Crispy Garlic Parmesan Edamame Snack

Serves: 4
Prep time: 10 minutes
Cook time: 12 minutes

Ingredients:
- 300g frozen edamame, thawed
- 2 tbsp olive oil
- 2 tbsp grated Parmesan cheese
- 1 tsp garlic powder
- 1/2 tsp onion powder
- Salt and black pepper, to taste

Preparation instructions:
1. Preheat the Ninja Dual Zone Air Fryer to 200°C for 5 minutes.
2. In a bowl, toss the thawed edamame with olive oil, Parmesan cheese, garlic powder, onion powder, salt, and black pepper.
3. Divide the seasoned edamame evenly between the two zones of the air fryer basket.
4. Air fry at 200°C for 12 minutes, shaking the basket halfway through, until the edamame is crispy and golden.
5. Remove from the air fryer and let cool for a few minutes before serving.

Cajun-Style Red Beans and Rice Fritters

Serves: 4
Prep time: 15 minutes
Cook time: 20 minutes

Ingredients:
- 200g cooked red beans
- 200g cooked rice
- 1 small onion, finely chopped
- 1 pepper, finely chopped
- 2 cloves garlic, minced
- 1 tsp Cajun seasoning
- 50g breadcrumbs
- 2 large eggs
- Salt and black pepper, to taste
- Cooking spray

Preparation instructions:
1. In a bowl, mash the cooked red beans and cooked rice together.
2. Add chopped onion, chopped pepper, minced garlic, Cajun seasoning, breadcrumbs, eggs, salt, and black pepper. Mix until well combined.
3. Preheat the Ninja Dual Zone Air Fryer to 190°C for 5 minutes.
4. Form the mixture into 12 fritters and place them on the air fryer tray.
5. Lightly spray the fritters with cooking spray.
6. Air fry at 190°C for 20 minutes, turning halfway through, until the fritters are golden brown and cooked through.
7. Allow them to cool for a few minutes before serving.

Mediterranean Stuffed Peppers with Quinoa

Serves: 4
Prep time: 20 minutes
Cook time: 25 minutes

Ingredients:
- 4 large peppers, halved and seeds removed
- 150g quinoa, cooked
- 100g cherry tomatoes, halved
- 50g Kalamata olives, chopped
- 50g feta cheese, crumbled
- 2 tbsp olive oil
- 1 tsp dried oregano
- Salt and black pepper, to taste
- Fresh parsley, for garnish

Preparation instructions:
1. Preheat the Ninja Dual Zone Air Fryer to 180°C for 5 minutes.
2. In a bowl, combine cooked quinoa, cherry tomatoes, chopped olives, feta cheese, olive oil, dried oregano, salt, and black pepper.
3. Stuff each pepper half with the quinoa mixture.
4. Place the stuffed peppers in the air fryer basket.
5. Air fry at 180°C for 25 minutes until the peppers are tender and slightly charred.
6. Garnish with fresh parsley and serve warm.

Panko-Crusted Falafel Nuggets

Serves: 4
Prep time: 15 minutes
Cook time: 15 minutes

Ingredients:
- 400g canned chickpeas, drained
- 2 cloves garlic, minced
- 1 tsp ground cumin
- 2 tbsp all-purpose flour
- Salt and black pepper, to taste
- 100g panko breadcrumbs
- Cooking spray
- 1 small onion, finely chopped
- 2 tbsp fresh parsley, chopped
- 1 tsp ground coriander

Preparation instructions:
1. Preheat the Ninja Dual Zone Air Fryer to 200°C for 5 minutes.
2. In a food processor, combine chickpeas, chopped onion, minced garlic, fresh parsley, ground cumin, ground coriander, all-purpose flour, salt, and black pepper. Pulse until well combined.
3. Shape the mixture into small nuggets.
4. Place panko breadcrumbs in a shallow bowl.
5. Roll each falafel nugget in the panko breadcrumbs, ensuring an even coating.
6. Lightly spray the nuggets with cooking spray.
7. Arrange the nuggets in the air fryer basket.
8. Air fry at 200°C for 15 minutes, turning halfway through, until golden brown and crispy.
9. Allow to cool for a few minutes before serving.

Air-Fried Butter Bean and Tomato Casserole

Serves: 4
Prep time: 10 minutes
Cook time: 20 minutes

Ingredients:
- 400g canned butter beans, drained and rinsed
- 200g cherry tomatoes, halved
- 1 small red onion, finely chopped
- 2 cloves garlic, minced
- 2 tbsp olive oil
- 1 tsp dried thyme
- 1 tsp smoked paprika
- Salt and black pepper, to taste
- Fresh basil, for garnish

Preparation instructions:
1. Preheat the Ninja Dual Zone Air Fryer to 180°C for 5 minutes.
2. In a bowl, combine butter beans, cherry tomatoes, chopped red onion, minced garlic, olive oil, dried thyme, smoked paprika, salt, and black pepper.
3. Transfer the mixture to the air fryer basket.
4. Air fry at 180°C for 20 minutes, stirring occasionally, until the tomatoes are soft and the flavours meld.
5. Garnish with fresh basil before serving.

Smoky BBQ Baked Beans with Bacon

Serves: 4
Prep time: 10 minutes
Cook time: 15 minutes

Ingredients:
- 400g canned baked beans
- 4 slices bacon, cooked and crumbled
- 3 tbsp barbecue sauce
- 1 tbsp brown sugar
- 1 tsp Dijon mustard
- 1/2 tsp liquid smoke (optional)
- Salt and black pepper, to taste

Preparation instructions:
1. Preheat the Ninja Dual Zone Air Fryer to 180°C for 5 minutes.
2. In a bowl, mix baked beans, crumbled bacon, barbecue sauce, brown sugar, Dijon mustard, liquid smoke (if using), salt, and black pepper.
3. Transfer the bean mixture to the air fryer basket.
4. Air fry at 180°C for 15 minutes, stirring halfway through, until the beans are hot and bubbly.
5. Let it cool for a few minutes before serving.

Harissa-Spiced Chickpea Fries

Serves: 4
Prep time: 15 minutes
Cook time: 15 minutes

Ingredients:
- 400g canned chickpeas, drained and rinsed
- 2 tbsp olive oil
- 1 tbsp harissa paste
- 1 tsp ground cumin
- 1 tsp smoked paprika
- Salt and black pepper, to taste
- 50g chickpea flour (besan)

Preparation instructions:
1. Preheat the Ninja Dual Zone Air Fryer to 200°C for 5 minutes.
2. In a bowl, toss chickpeas with olive oil, harissa paste, ground cumin, smoked paprika, salt, and black pepper.
3. Coat the chickpeas evenly with chickpea flour.
4. Place the chickpeas in one zone of the air fryer basket.
5. Air fry at 200°C for 15 minutes, shaking the basket halfway through, until the chickpeas are crispy.
6. Let them cool for a few minutes before serving.

Kidney Bean and Vegetable Stuffed Mushrooms

Serves: 4
Prep time: 20 minutes
Cook time: 15 minutes

Ingredients:
- 200g kidney beans, cooked and mashed
- 4 large portobello mushrooms, stems removed
- 1 small red onion, finely chopped
- 1 pepper, diced
- 2 cloves garlic, minced
- 2 tbsp olive oil
- 1 tsp dried oregano
- 1 tsp smoked paprika
- Salt and black pepper, to taste
- 100g vegan cheese, grated

Preparation instructions:
1. Preheat the Ninja Dual Zone Air Fryer to 180°C for 5 minutes.
2. In a pan, sauté red onion, pepper, and garlic in olive oil until softened.
3. Add mashed kidney beans, dried oregano, smoked paprika, salt, and black pepper. Cook for another 2 minutes.
4. Stuff each mushroom cap with the kidney bean mixture.
5. Sprinkle grated vegan cheese over the stuffed mushrooms.
6. Place the mushrooms in the other zone of the air fryer basket.
7. Air fry at 180°C for 15 minutes or until the mushrooms are tender and the cheese is melted.
8. Allow them to cool slightly before serving.

Turmeric and Cumin-Spiced Lentil Chips

Serves: 4
Prep time: 15 minutes
Cook time: 15 minutes

Ingredients:
- 200g dried green lentils, cooked and mashed
- 2 tbsp olive oil
- 1 tsp ground turmeric
- 1 tsp ground cumin
- 1 tsp garlic powder
- Salt and black pepper, to taste
- 50g gram flour (besan)

Preparation instructions:
1. Preheat the Ninja Dual Zone Air Fryer to 200°C for 5 minutes.
2. In a bowl, combine mashed lentils with olive oil, ground turmeric, ground cumin, garlic powder, salt, and black pepper.
3. Mix in gram flour until a dough-like consistency is formed.
4. Shape the lentil mixture into chips.
5. Place the lentil chips in one zone of the air fryer basket.
6. Air fry at 200°C for 15 minutes, turning halfway through, until the chips are golden and crispy.
7. Let them cool a bit before serving.

Black-Eyed Pea and Vegetable Patties

Serves: 4
Prep time: 15 minutes
Cook time: 15 minutes

Ingredients:
- 200g canned black-eyed peas, drained and mashed
- 1 medium carrot, grated
- 1 courgette, grated
- 1 small red onion, finely chopped
- 2 cloves garlic, minced
- 2 tbsp fresh parsley, chopped
- 50g breadcrumbs
- 1 tsp ground cumin
- 1/2 tsp smoked paprika
- Salt and black pepper, to taste
- 2 tbsp olive oil (for air frying)

Preparation instructions:
1. Preheat the Ninja Dual Zone Air Fryer to 200°C for 5 minutes.
2. In a bowl, combine mashed black-eyed peas, grated carrot, grated courgette, chopped red onion, minced garlic, fresh parsley, breadcrumbs, ground cumin, smoked paprika, salt, and black pepper.
3. Form the mixture into patties.
4. Brush the patties with olive oil.
5. Place the patties in one zone of the air fryer basket.
6. Air fry at 200°C for 15 minutes, flipping halfway through, until the patties are golden and crispy.
7. Let them cool slightly before serving.

Air-Fried Chickpea and Sweet Potato Tacos

Serves: 4
Prep time: 20 minutes
Cook time: 15 minutes

Ingredients:
- 200g canned chickpeas, drained
- 1 large sweet potato, peeled and diced
- 1 tbsp olive oil
- 1 tsp ground cumin
- 1 tsp smoked paprika
- 1/2 tsp chilli powder
- Salt and black pepper, to taste
- 8 small taco shells
- 1 avocado, sliced
- 50g red cabbage, shredded
- Fresh coriander, for garnish

Preparation instructions:
1. Preheat the Ninja Dual Zone Air Fryer to 200°C for 5 minutes.
2. In a bowl, toss chickpeas and diced sweet potato with olive oil, ground cumin, smoked paprika, chilli powder, salt, and black pepper.
3. Place the mixture in one zone of the air fryer basket.
4. Air fry at 200°C for 15 minutes, shaking the basket halfway through, until the sweet potatoes are tender and chickpeas are crispy.
5. Warm the taco shells in the other zone of the air fryer basket for the last 3 minutes.
6. Assemble the tacos with the air-fried chickpeas and sweet potatoes, sliced avocado, shredded red cabbage, and garnish with fresh coriander.

Warm Herbed Cannellini Bean Salad

Serves: 4
Prep time: 15 minutes
Cook time: 5 minutes

Ingredients:
- 400g canned cannellini beans, drained and rinsed
- 1 cucumber, diced
- 200g cherry tomatoes, halved
- 50g fresh mint, chopped
- 60g fresh parsley, chopped
- 100g feta cheese, crumbled
- 2 tbsp extra virgin olive oil
- 1 tbsp red wine vinegar
- Salt and black pepper, to taste

Preparation instructions:
1. In a large bowl, combine cannellini beans, diced cucumber, cherry tomatoes, fresh mint, fresh parsley, and crumbled feta.
2. In a small bowl, whisk together extra virgin olive oil, red wine vinegar, salt, and black pepper.
3. Drizzle the dressing over the bean mixture and toss gently to combine.
4. Warm the salad in the Ninja Dual Zone Air Fryer at a low temperature for 5 minutes.
5. Serve immediately, enjoying the warm and flavorful combination, or refrigerate until ready to serve.

CHAPTER 8
Healthy Vegetables and Sides

Sesame Soy Air-Fried Broccoli Bites

Serves: 4
Prep time: 10 minutes
Cook time: 15 minutes

Ingredients:
- 300g broccoli florets
- 2 tbsp soy sauce
- 1 tbsp sesame oil
- 1 tbsp olive oil
- 1 tsp sesame seeds
- 1/4 tsp garlic powder
- Salt and black pepper, to taste

Preparation instructions:
1. Preheat the Ninja Dual Zone Air Fryer to 180°C for 5 minutes.
2. In a bowl, toss broccoli florets with soy sauce, sesame oil, olive oil, sesame seeds, garlic powder, salt, and black pepper.
3. Divide the seasoned broccoli evenly between the air fryer baskets.
4. Air fry at 180°C for 15 minutes or until the broccoli is crispy and golden.
5. Shake the baskets halfway through for even cooking.
6. Remove from the air fryer and serve immediately, providing a delightful crunch in every bite.

Turmeric Roasted Cauliflower Steaks

Serves: 4
Prep time: 10 minutes
Cook time: 20 minutes

Ingredients:
- 1 large cauliflower, sliced into steaks
- 2 tbsp olive oil
- 1 tsp turmeric powder
- 1 tsp cumin
- 1/2 tsp smoked paprika
- Salt and black pepper, to taste

Preparation instructions:
1. Preheat the Ninja Dual Zone Air Fryer to 200°C for 5 minutes.
2. In a bowl, mix olive oil, turmeric powder, cumin, smoked paprika, salt, and black pepper.
3. Brush the cauliflower steaks with the turmeric mixture, ensuring even coverage.
4. Place the steaks in the air fryer baskets.
5. Air fry at 200°C for 20 minutes or until the cauliflower is tender and golden brown.
6. Flip the steaks halfway through for uniform roasting.
7. Serve the turmeric-roasted cauliflower steaks hot, providing a flavorful and vibrant dish.

Parmesan Courgette Crisps with Basil Dip

Serves: 4
Prep time: 10 minutes
Cook time: 12 minutes

Ingredients:
- 2 large courgettes, thinly sliced
- 50g Parmesan cheese, grated
- 2 tbsp olive oil
- 25g fresh basil leaves, chopped
- 120ml Greek yoghurt
- 1 tbsp lemon juice
- Salt and black pepper, to taste

Preparation instructions:
1. Preheat the Ninja Dual Zone Air Fryer to 190°C for 5 minutes.
2. In a bowl, toss courgette slices with Parmesan and olive oil until coated.
3. Arrange the coated courgette slices in the air fryer baskets.
4. Air fry at 190°C for 12 minutes or until the crisps are golden and crispy.
5. Meanwhile, in another bowl, mix chopped basil, Greek yoghurt, lemon juice, salt, and black pepper to prepare the dip.
6. Serve the Parmesan courgette crisps with the basil dip for a delightful and crunchy snack.

Spiced Carrot and Chickpea Fritters

Serves: 4
Prep time: 15 minutes
Cook time: 12 minutes

Ingredients:
- 300g carrots, grated
- 200g canned chickpeas, drained and mashed
- 45g fresh coriander, chopped
- 50g red onion, finely chopped
- 2 tbsp gram flour
- 1 tsp cumin powder
- 1/2 tsp coriander powder
- 1/4 tsp cayenne pepper
- Salt and black pepper, to taste
- 2 tbsp olive oil (for air frying)

Preparation instructions:
1. Preheat the Ninja Dual Zone Air Fryer to 200°C for 5 minutes.
2. In a bowl, combine grated carrots, mashed chickpeas, fresh coriander, red onion, gram flour, cumin powder, coriander powder, cayenne pepper, salt, and black pepper.
3. Shape the mixture into fritters and place them in the air fryer baskets.
4. Brush the fritters with olive oil for a crispy finish.
5. Air fry at 200°C for 12 minutes or until the fritters are golden brown and cooked through.
6. Serve the spiced carrot and chickpea fritters hot, offering a delightful blend of flavours and textures.

Garlic Brussels Sprouts Chips

Serves: 4
Prep time: 10 minutes
Cook time: 15 minutes

Ingredients:
- 400g Brussels sprouts, trimmed and halved
- 2 tbsp olive oil
- 3 cloves garlic, minced
- Salt and black pepper, to taste
- 60g grated Parmesan cheese

Preparation instructions:
1. Preheat the Ninja Dual Zone Air Fryer to 180°C for 5 minutes.
2. In a bowl, toss Brussels sprouts with olive oil, minced garlic, salt, and black pepper.
3. Arrange the Brussels sprouts in the air fryer baskets.
4. Air fry at 180°C for 15 minutes or until the chips are crispy and lightly browned.
5. Sprinkle grated Parmesan cheese over the chips and air fry for an additional 2 minutes.
6. Serve the garlic Brussels sprouts chips hot, providing a flavorful and satisfying snack.

Cumin-Spiced Sweet Potato Wedges

Serves: 4
Prep time: 12 minutes
Cook time: 20 minutes

Ingredients:
- 600g sweet potatoes, cut into wedges
- 2 tbsp olive oil
- 1 tsp ground cumin
- 1/2 tsp smoked paprika
- 1/4 tsp cayenne pepper
- Salt and black pepper, to taste

Preparation instructions:
1. Preheat the Ninja Dual Zone Air Fryer to 200°C for 5 minutes.
2. In a bowl, toss sweet potato wedges with olive oil, ground cumin, smoked paprika, cayenne pepper, salt, and black pepper.
3. Place the wedges in the air fryer baskets.
4. Air fry at 200°C for 20 minutes or until the sweet potato wedges are tender and crispy.
5. Serve the cumin-spiced sweet potato wedges hot, delivering a perfect balance of spices and textures.

Mediterranean Stuffed Mushrooms with Quinoa

Serves: 4
Prep time: 15 minutes
Cook time: 12 minutes

Ingredients:
- 200g mushrooms, stems removed and reserved
- 100g quinoa, cooked
- 50g cherry tomatoes, diced
- 50g black olives, chopped
- 50g feta cheese, crumbled
- 2 tbsp fresh parsley, chopped
- 2 tbsp olive oil
- 1 clove garlic, minced
- Salt and black pepper, to taste

Preparation instructions:
1. Preheat the Ninja Dual Zone Air Fryer to 180°C for 5 minutes.
2. In a bowl, mix cooked quinoa, diced cherry tomatoes, chopped black olives, feta cheese, fresh parsley, olive oil, minced garlic, salt, and black pepper.
3. Stuff each mushroom cap with the quinoa mixture, using the reserved mushroom stems.
4. Arrange the stuffed mushrooms in the air fryer baskets.
5. Air fry at 180°C for 12 minutes or until the mushrooms are tender and the filling is golden.
6. Serve the Mediterranean stuffed mushrooms hot, offering a delightful combination of flavours.

Lemon Dill Air-Fried Asparagus Spears

Serves: 4
Prep time: 10 minutes
Cook time: 8 minutes

Ingredients:
- 300g asparagus spears, trimmed
- 2 tbsp olive oil
- 1 lemon, zest and juice
- 1 tbsp fresh dill, chopped
- Salt and black pepper, to taste

Preparation instructions:
1. Preheat the Ninja Dual Zone Air Fryer to 200°C for 5 minutes.
2. In a bowl, toss asparagus spears with olive oil, lemon zest, lemon juice, fresh dill, salt, and black pepper.
3. Arrange the asparagus spears in the air fryer baskets.
4. Air fry at 200°C for 8 minutes or until the asparagus is tender-crisp.
5. Serve the lemon dill air-fried asparagus spears hot, providing a zesty and herb-infused side.

Cheesy Cauliflower Bites with Yoghurt Dip

Serves: 4
Prep time: 15 minutes
Cook time: 15 minutes

Ingredients:
- 400g cauliflower florets
- 100g breadcrumbs
- 100g grated cheddar cheese
- 2 eggs, beaten
- 1 tsp garlic powder
- 1 tsp onion powder
- Salt and black pepper, to taste
- Olive oil (for greasing)

Preparation instructions:
1. Preheat the Ninja Dual Zone Air Fryer to 190°C for 5 minutes.
2. In a bowl, combine cauliflower florets, breadcrumbs, grated cheddar cheese, beaten eggs, garlic powder, onion powder, salt, and black pepper.
3. Shape the mixture into bite-sized cauliflower balls.
4. Grease the air fryer baskets with olive oil and place the cauliflower bites inside.
5. Air fry at 190°C for 15 minutes or until the bites are golden brown and crispy.
6. Serve the cheesy cauliflower bites hot, accompanied by a refreshing yoghurt dip.

Pesto Parmesan Aubergine Slices

Serves: 4
Prep time: 15 minutes
Cook time: 12 minutes

Ingredients:
- 1 large aubergine, sliced into rounds
- 60g pesto sauce
- 50g Parmesan cheese, grated
- 2 tbsp olive oil
- 1/2 tsp garlic powder
- Salt and black pepper, to taste
- Fresh basil leaves for garnish (optional)

Preparation instructions:
1. Preheat the Ninja Dual Zone Air Fryer to 200°C for 5 minutes.
2. In a bowl, coat aubergine slices with pesto sauce, grated Parmesan cheese, olive oil, garlic powder, salt, and black pepper.
3. Arrange the coated aubergine slices in the air fryer baskets.
4. Air fry at 200°C for 12 minutes or until the aubergine is golden and tender.
5. Garnish with fresh basil leaves if desired.
6. Serve the Pesto Parmesan Aubergine Slices hot as a flavorful side dish.

Crispy Rosemary and Garlic Fries

Serves: 4
Prep time: 15 minutes
Cook time: 20 minutes

Ingredients:
- 600g potatoes, cut into fries
- 3 tbsp olive oil
- 2 tbsp fresh rosemary, chopped
- 2 cloves garlic, minced
- Salt and black pepper, to taste
- 30g Parmesan cheese, grated (optional)

Preparation instructions:
1. Preheat the Ninja Dual Zone Air Fryer to 190°C for 5 minutes.
2. In a bowl, toss potato fries with olive oil, chopped rosemary, minced garlic, salt, and black pepper.
3. Arrange the seasoned fries in the air fryer baskets.
4. Air fry at 190°C for 20 minutes or until the fries are crispy and golden.
5. Sprinkle with grated Parmesan cheese if desired.
6. Serve the Crispy Rosemary and Garlic Fries hot, offering a delightful aroma and crunch.

Honey Balsamic Glazed Beetroot Slices

Serves: 4
Prep time: 10 minutes
Cook time: 15 minutes

Ingredients:
- 400g beetroot, thinly sliced
- 2 tbsp honey
- 2 tbsp balsamic vinegar
- 2 tbsp olive oil
- Salt and black pepper, to taste
- Fresh thyme leaves for garnish (optional)

Preparation instructions:
1. Preheat the Ninja Dual Zone Air Fryer to 180°C for 5 minutes.
2. In a bowl, combine beetroot slices with honey, balsamic vinegar, olive oil, salt, and black pepper.
3. Arrange the glazed beetroot slices in the air fryer baskets.
4. Air fry at 180°C for 15 minutes or until the beetroot is tender and glazed.
5. Garnish with fresh thyme leaves if desired.
6. Serve the Honey Balsamic Glazed Beetroot Slices hot, providing a sweet and tangy side dish.

Herb-Roasted Butternut Squash Cubes

Serves: 4
Prep time: 15 minutes
Cook time: 20 minutes

Ingredients:
- 500g butternut squash, peeled and cubed
- 2 tbsp olive oil
- 1 tsp dried thyme
- 1 tsp dried rosemary
- 1/2 tsp garlic powder
- Salt and black pepper, to taste
- Fresh parsley for garnish (optional)

Preparation instructions:
1. Preheat the Ninja Dual Zone Air Fryer to 200°C for 5 minutes.
2. In a bowl, toss butternut squash cubes with olive oil, dried thyme, dried rosemary, garlic powder, salt, and black pepper.
3. Divide the seasoned squash evenly between the air fryer baskets.
4. Air fry at 200°C for 20 minutes or until the squash is tender and golden.
5. Garnish with fresh parsley if desired.
6. Serve the Herb-Roasted Butternut Squash Cubes as a delightful side dish.

Tomato Basil Caprese Stuffed Sweet Potatoes

Serves: 4
Prep time: 15 minutes
Cook time: 25 minutes

Ingredients:
- 4 medium sweet potatoes
- 200g cherry tomatoes, halved
- 150g fresh mozzarella, diced
- 30g fresh basil, chopped
- 2 tbsp balsamic glaze
- 2 tbsp olive oil
- Salt and black pepper, to taste

Preparation instructions:
1. Preheat the Ninja Dual Zone Air Fryer to 200°C for 5 minutes.
2. Pierce sweet potatoes with a fork and place them in the air fryer baskets.
3. Air fry at 200°C for 25 minutes or until sweet potatoes are tender.
4. In a bowl, combine cherry tomatoes, fresh mozzarella, fresh basil, olive oil, salt, and black pepper.
5. Once sweet potatoes are cooked, slice them open and stuff with the tomato-basil mixture.
6. Drizzle with balsamic glaze before serving.
7. Serve the Tomato Basil Caprese Stuffed Sweet Potatoes for a flavorful and vibrant dish.

Curry-Spiced Squash Rings

Serves: 4
Prep time: 10 minutes
Cook time: 15 minutes

Ingredients:
- 1 small acorn squash, sliced into rings
- 2 tbsp olive oil
- 1 tsp curry powder
- 1/2 tsp ground cumin
- 1/2 tsp turmeric
- 1/4 tsp cayenne pepper
- Salt and black pepper, to taste
- Fresh coriander for garnish (optional)

Preparation instructions:
1. Preheat the Ninja Dual Zone Air Fryer to 190°C for 5 minutes.
2. In a bowl, toss acorn squash rings with olive oil, curry powder, ground cumin, turmeric, cayenne pepper, salt, and black pepper.
3. Arrange the seasoned squash rings in the air fryer baskets.
4. Air fry at 190°C for 15 minutes or until the squash is tender and slightly crispy.
5. Garnish with fresh coriander if desired.
6. Serve the Curry-Spiced Squash Rings as a unique and flavorful side dish.

CHAPTER 9
Family Favourites

Air-Fried Chicken and Waffle Sliders

Serves: 4
Prep time: 15 minutes
Cook time: 20 minutes

Ingredients:
- 400g chicken tenders
- 100g cheddar cheese, shredded
- 1 tbsp olive oil
- 1/2 tsp onion powder
- Salt and black pepper, to taste
- Fresh chives for garnish (optional)
- 200g waffle squares, toasted
- 60ml maple syrup
- 1/2 tsp garlic powder

Preparation instructions:
1. Preheat the Ninja Dual Zone Air Fryer to 200°C for 5 minutes.
2. In a bowl, toss chicken tenders with olive oil, garlic powder, onion powder, salt, and black pepper.
3. Place the seasoned chicken tenders in one zone of the air fryer basket.
4. In the other zone, arrange the waffle squares.
5. Air fry at 200°C for 20 minutes or until the chicken is cooked through and the waffles are crispy.
6. During the last 5 minutes, sprinkle shredded cheddar over the chicken tenders to melt.
7. Assemble sliders by placing a chicken tender on a waffle square, drizzle with maple syrup, and garnish with fresh chives if desired.
8. Serve the Air-Fried Chicken and Waffle Sliders for a delightful twist on a classic.

Cheesy Potato and Bacon Croquettes

Serves: 4
Prep time: 20 minutes
Cook time: 15 minutes

Ingredients:
- 400g mashed potatoes, cooled
- 100g cheddar cheese, grated
- 8 slices bacon, cooked and crumbled
- 60g breadcrumbs
- 1 egg, beaten
- 2 tbsp fresh parsley, chopped
- 1/2 tsp garlic powder
- Salt and black pepper, to taste
- Cooking spray

Preparation instructions:
1. Preheat the Ninja Dual Zone Air Fryer to 190°C for 5 minutes.
2. In a bowl, combine mashed potatoes, cheddar cheese, bacon, breadcrumbs, beaten egg, fresh parsley, garlic powder, salt, and black pepper.
3. Shape the mixture into small croquettes.
4. Place the croquettes in one zone of the air fryer basket, ensuring they are not touching.
5. Air fry at 190°C for 15 minutes or until golden and crispy, turning halfway through.
6. Serve the Cheesy Potato and Bacon Croquettes as a tasty appetisers or side dish.

Mini Beef and Veggie Pies with Puff Pastry

Serves: 4
Prep time: 25 minutes
Cook time: 20 minutes

Ingredients:
- 300g lean ground beef
- 1 carrot, diced
- 2 tbsp tomato paste
- 1/2 tsp dried thyme
- 1 sheet puff pastry, thawed
- 1 onion, finely chopped
- 1 courgette, diced
- 1 tsp Worcestershire sauce
- Salt and black pepper, to taste
- 1 egg, beaten
- Fresh parsley for garnish (optional)

Preparation instructions:
1. Preheat the Ninja Dual Zone Air Fryer to 180°C for 5 minutes.
2. In a pan, brown ground beef with onion, carrot, and courgette until vegetables are tender.
3. Stir in tomato paste, Worcestershire sauce, dried thyme, salt, and black pepper.
4. Roll out puff pastry and cut into 4 squares.
5. Place each pastry square in one zone of the air fryer basket.
6. Spoon the beef and veggie mixture onto one half of each pastry square.
7. Fold the other half of the pastry over the filling, creating mini pies.
8. Seal the edges with a fork and brush the tops with beaten egg.
9. Air fry at 180°C for 20 minutes or until the pastry is golden and flaky.
10. Garnish with fresh parsley if desired.
11. Serve the Mini Beef and Veggie Pies with Puff Pastry as a delightful and satisfying meal.

Crispy Garlic Parmesan Chicken Strips

Serves: 4
Prep time: 15 minutes
Cook time: 12 minutes

Ingredients:
- 400g chicken breast, cut into strips
- 100g breadcrumbs
- 50g grated Parmesan cheese
- 1 tsp garlic powder
- 1/2 tsp onion powder
- Salt and black pepper, to taste
- 2 eggs, beaten
- Cooking spray

Preparation instructions:
1. Preheat the Ninja Dual Zone Air Fryer to 200°C for 5 minutes.
2. In a bowl, combine breadcrumbs, grated Parmesan, garlic powder, onion powder, salt, and black pepper.
3. Dip each chicken strip into beaten eggs, then coat with the breadcrumb mixture.
4. Place the coated chicken strips in one zone of the air fryer basket, ensuring they are not touching.
5. Lightly spray the chicken strips with cooking spray.
6. Air fry at 200°C for 12 minutes or until golden brown and crispy, turning halfway through.

Baked Beans and Sausage Stuffed Peppers

Serves: 4
Prep time: 20 minutes
Cook time: 25 minutes

Ingredients:
- 4 large peppers, halved and deseeded
- 400g canned baked beans
- 8 cooked sausage links, chopped
- 1 onion, finely chopped
- 1 garlic clove, minced
- 200g cheddar cheese, shredded
- 2 tbsp tomato paste
- 1 tsp dried oregano
- Salt and black pepper, to taste
- Fresh parsley for garnish (optional)

Preparation instructions:
1. Preheat the Ninja Dual Zone Air Fryer to 180°C for 5 minutes.
2. In a bowl, mix together baked beans, chopped sausage, onion, garlic, cheddar cheese, tomato paste, dried oregano, salt, and black pepper.
3. Stuff each pepper half with the bean and sausage mixture.
4. Place the stuffed peppers in one zone of the air fryer basket.
5. Air fry at 180°C for 25 minutes or until the peppers are tender and the filling is heated through.
6. Garnish with fresh parsley if desired.

Air-Fried Mac and Cheese Bites

Serves: 4
Prep time: 15 minutes
Cook time: 10 minutes

Ingredients:
- 200g elbow macaroni, cooked and cooled
- 100g cheddar cheese, shredded
- 50g Parmesan cheese, grated
- 2 eggs
- 60ml whole milk
- 1/4 tsp garlic powder
- 1/4 tsp onion powder
- Salt and black pepper, to taste
- 100g breadcrumbs

Preparation instructions:
1. Preheat the Ninja Dual Zone Air Fryer to 190°C for 5 minutes.
2. In a bowl, combine cooked macaroni, cheddar cheese, Parmesan cheese, eggs, whole milk, garlic powder, onion powder, salt, and black pepper.
3. Shape the mixture into small mac and cheese bites.
4. Roll each bite in breadcrumbs, ensuring they are coated evenly.
5. Place the bites in one zone of the air fryer basket, leaving space between them.
6. Air fry at 190°C for 10 minutes or until golden and crispy.

Sweet and Sour Chicken Stir-Fry

Serves: 4
Prep time: 15 minutes
Cook time: 12 minutes

Ingredients:
- 400g chicken breast, thinly sliced
- 200g pineapple chunks, fresh or canned
- 1 red pepper, sliced
- 1 green pepper, sliced
- 1 onion, thinly sliced
- 60ml soy sauce
- 30ml rice vinegar
- 2 tbsp tomato ketchup
- 2 tbsp brown sugar
- 1 tbsp cornstarch
- 1 tbsp vegetable oil
- Sesame seeds and chopped green onions for garnish (optional)

Preparation instructions:
1. Preheat the Ninja Dual Zone Air Fryer to 200°C for 5 minutes.
2. In a bowl, mix together soy sauce, rice vinegar, tomato ketchup, brown sugar, and cornstarch to create the sauce.
3. Heat vegetable oil in one zone of the air fryer basket.
4. Stir-fry chicken slices until browned and cooked through.
5. Add pineapple, peppers, and onion to the air fryer basket with chicken.
6. Pour the sauce over the ingredients and toss to coat evenly.
7. Air fry at 200°C for 12 minutes or until the vegetables are tender and the sauce thickens.
8. Garnish with sesame seeds and chopped green onions if desired.

Meatball Sub Skewers with Marinara Dipping Sauce

Serves: 4
Prep time: 20 minutes
Cook time: 15 minutes

Ingredients:
- 400g ground beef
- 120g breadcrumbs
- 60g grated Parmesan cheese
- 1 large egg
- 2 cloves garlic, minced
- 1 tsp dried oregano
- 1 tsp dried basil
- Salt and black pepper, to taste
- 200ml marinara sauce
- 4 sub rolls, cut into bite-sized pieces

Preparation instructions:
1. Preheat the Ninja Dual Zone Air Fryer to 180°C for 5 minutes.
2. In a bowl, combine ground beef, breadcrumbs, Parmesan cheese, egg, garlic, oregano, basil, salt, and black pepper to form meatballs.
3. Shape the meat mixture into small meatballs.
4. Place meatballs in one zone of the air fryer basket.
5. Air fry at 180°C for 15 minutes or until meatballs are browned and cooked through.
6. Thread meatballs onto skewers alternately with bite-sized pieces of sub rolls.
7. Heat marinara sauce in the other zone of the air fryer basket for dipping.
8. Serve meatball sub skewers with marinara dipping sauce.

Air-Fried Chicken and Vegetable Spring Rolls

Serves: 4
Prep time: 25 minutes
Cook time: 15 minutes

Ingredients:
- 200g cooked chicken, shredded
- 100g cabbage, finely shredded
- 100g carrots, julienned
- 50g bean sprouts
- 2 spring onions, sliced
- 2 tbsp soy sauce
- 1 tbsp oyster sauce
- 1 tsp sesame oil
- 12 spring roll wrappers
- Cooking spray

Preparation instructions:
1. Preheat the Ninja Dual Zone Air Fryer to 200°C for 5 minutes.
2. In a bowl, combine shredded chicken, cabbage, carrots, bean sprouts, spring onions, soy sauce, oyster sauce, and sesame oil.
3. Place a portion of the mixture onto each spring roll wrapper and roll tightly.
4. Lightly spray the spring rolls with cooking spray.
5. Arrange the spring rolls in one zone of the air fryer basket.
6. Air fry at 200°C for 15 minutes or until the spring rolls are golden and crispy.
7. Serve with your favourite dipping sauce.

Family-Style Chicken and Veggie Quesadillas

Serves: 4
Prep time: 15 minutes
Cook time: 10 minutes

Ingredients:
- 400g chicken breast, cooked and shredded
- 1 red pepper, diced
- 1 green pepper, diced
- 1 onion, finely chopped
- 200g cheddar cheese, grated
- 4 large flour tortillas
- 1 tsp ground cumin
- 1 tsp paprika
- 1/2 tsp chilli powder
- Salt and black pepper, to taste
- Cooking spray

Preparation instructions:
1. Preheat the Ninja Dual Zone Air Fryer to 200°C for 5 minutes.
2. In one zone, sauté diced peppers and onions until softened.
3. In the other zone, place one tortilla and spread a layer of shredded chicken.
4. Add sautéed peppers and onions on top of the chicken.
5. Sprinkle grated cheddar cheese and season with ground cumin, paprika, chilli powder, salt, and black pepper.
6. Place another tortilla on top, creating a quesadilla.
7. Repeat the process for the remaining tortillas.
8. Lightly spray both sides of the quesadillas with cooking spray.
9. Air fry at 200°C for 10 minutes or until the quesadillas are golden and crispy.
10. Allow to cool slightly before slicing into wedges.

Veggie-Packed Air-Fried Chicken Burgers

Serves: 4
Prep time: 20 minutes
Cook time: 15 minutes

Ingredients:
- 400g ground chicken
- 1 carrot, grated
- 1/2 red onion, finely chopped
- 2 cloves garlic, minced
- 1 tsp dried oregano
- 1 tsp smoked paprika
- Salt and black pepper, to taste
- 4 whole wheat burger buns
- Lettuce, tomato slices, and condiments for serving
- 1 courgette, grated

Preparation instructions:
1. Preheat the Ninja Dual Zone Air Fryer to 180°C for 5 minutes.
2. In a bowl, combine ground chicken, grated courgette, grated carrot, chopped red onion, minced garlic, dried oregano, smoked paprika, salt, and black pepper.
3. Shape the mixture into four burger patties.
4. Place the burger patties in one zone of the air fryer basket.
5. Air fry at 180°C for 15 minutes or until the burgers are cooked through and browned.
6. Toast the whole wheat burger buns in the other zone.
7. Assemble the burgers with lettuce, tomato slices, and your favourite condiments.

Cheddar and Onion Stuffed Mushrooms

Serves: 4
Prep time: 12 minutes
Cook time: 8 minutes

Ingredients:
- 16 large mushrooms, stems removed
- 100g cheddar cheese, grated
- 1 onion, finely chopped
- 2 tbsp breadcrumbs
- 2 tbsp fresh parsley, chopped
- 2 tbsp olive oil
- Salt and black pepper, to taste

Preparation instructions:
1. Preheat the Ninja Dual Zone Air Fryer to 180°C for 5 minutes.
2. In a bowl, mix grated cheddar cheese, chopped onion, breadcrumbs, fresh parsley, olive oil, salt, and black pepper.
3. Stuff each mushroom cap with the cheddar and onion mixture.
4. Arrange the stuffed mushrooms in one zone of the air fryer basket.
5. Air fry at 180°C for 8 minutes or until the mushrooms are tender and the cheese is melted.
6. Serve immediately, garnished with additional fresh parsley if desired.

Homemade Chicken Nuggets with Honey Mustard Dip

Serves: 4
Prep time: 15 minutes
Cook time: 12 minutes

Ingredients:
- 400g boneless, skinless chicken breasts, cut into bite-sized pieces
- 100g breadcrumbs
- 50g grated Parmesan cheese
- 1 tsp garlic powder
- 1 tsp onion powder
- Salt and black pepper, to taste
- 2 large eggs, beaten
- Cooking spray

Preparation instructions:
1. Preheat the Ninja Dual Zone Air Fryer to 200°C for 5 minutes.
2. In a bowl, combine breadcrumbs, grated Parmesan cheese, garlic powder, onion powder, salt, and black pepper.
3. Dip each chicken piece into beaten eggs, then coat with the breadcrumb mixture.
4. Arrange the coated chicken pieces in one zone of the air fryer basket.
5. Lightly spray with cooking spray.
6. Air fry at 200°C for 12 minutes or until the chicken nuggets are golden and cooked through.
7. Serve hot with honey mustard dip.

Sausage and Pea Pastry Parcels

Serves: 4
Prep time: 20 minutes
Cook time: 15 minutes

Ingredients:
- 8 pork sausages
- 200g frozen peas, thawed
- 1 sheet puff pastry, thawed
- 1 egg, beaten (for egg wash)
- Salt and black pepper, to taste
- Tomato chutney (for serving)

Preparation instructions:
1. Preheat the Ninja Dual Zone Air Fryer to 180°C for 5 minutes.
2. Cook the sausages in one zone until browned and cooked through.
3. In the other zone, air fry the thawed peas until slightly crispy.
4. Roll out the puff pastry and cut into 4 squares.
5. Place a cooked sausage on each pastry square and top with crispy peas.
6. Season with salt and black pepper.
7. Fold the pastry to enclose the filling, creating parcels.
8. Brush each parcel with beaten egg for a golden finish.
9. Air fry at 180°C for 15 minutes or until the pastry is puffed and golden.
10. Serve with tomato chutney.

BBQ Pulled Pork Loaded Potato Skins

Serves: 4
Prep time: 15 minutes
Cook time: 25 minutes

Ingredients:
- 4 large baking potatoes, scrubbed
- 300g pulled pork (pre-cooked)
- 100g shredded cheddar cheese
- 4 tbsp BBQ sauce
- 2 spring onions, chopped
- Salt and black pepper, to taste
- Sour cream (for serving)

Preparation instructions:
1. Preheat the Ninja Dual Zone Air Fryer to 200°C for 5 minutes.
2. Pierce each potato several times with a fork and microwave for 10 minutes or until partially cooked.
3. Cut each potato in half lengthwise and scoop out the flesh, leaving a potato skin shell.
4. In one zone, air fry the potato skins until crispy.
5. In the other zone, mix pulled pork with BBQ sauce and heat until warmed through.
6. Fill each crispy potato skin with the pulled pork mixture.
7. Top with shredded cheddar cheese and air fry for an additional 5 minutes or until the cheese is melted and bubbly.
8. Garnish with chopped spring onions, season with salt and black pepper, and serve with a dollop of sour cream.

CHAPTER 10
Appetisers

Spinach and Mozzarella Stuffed Mushrooms

Serves: 4
Prep time: 15 minutes
Cook time: 12 minutes

Ingredients:
- 200g fresh mushrooms, stems removed
- 100g fresh spinach, chopped
- 100g mozzarella cheese, shredded
- 2 cloves garlic, minced
- 2 tbsp olive oil
- Salt and black pepper, to taste

Preparation instructions:
1. Preheat the Ninja Dual Zone Air Fryer to 180°C for 5 minutes.
2. In a bowl, mix chopped spinach, shredded mozzarella, minced garlic, salt, and black pepper.
3. Stuff each mushroom cap with the spinach and mozzarella mixture.
4. Place the stuffed mushrooms in one zone of the air fryer basket.
5. Drizzle olive oil over the stuffed mushrooms.
6. Air fry at 180°C for 12 minutes or until the mushrooms are tender and the cheese is melted and golden.
7. Serve hot.

Crispy Air-Fried Bruschetta Bites

Serves: 4
Prep time: 10 minutes
Cook time: 8 minutes

Ingredients:
- 4 slices baguette, thinly sliced
- 2 large tomatoes, diced
- 40g fresh basil, chopped
- 2 cloves garlic, minced
- 2 tbsp balsamic glaze
- 2 tbsp olive oil
- Salt and black pepper, to taste

Preparation instructions:
1. Preheat the Ninja Dual Zone Air Fryer to 200°C for 5 minutes.
2. In a bowl, combine diced tomatoes, chopped basil, minced garlic, balsamic glaze, olive oil, salt, and black pepper.
3. Brush baguette slices with olive oil on both sides.
4. Arrange the baguette slices in one zone of the air fryer basket.
5. Air fry at 200°C for 4 minutes, flipping halfway through, until the baguette slices are golden and crispy.
6. Top each crispy baguette slice with the tomato and basil mixture.
7. Air fry for an additional 4 minutes.
8. Serve immediately.

Thai Chicken Satay Skewers

Serves: 4
Prep time: 20 minutes
Cook time: 12 minutes

Ingredients:
- 400g boneless, skinless chicken thighs, cut into strips
- 4 tbsp soy sauce
- 2 tbsp coconut milk
- 1 tbsp red curry paste
- 1 tbsp honey
- 1 tbsp lime juice
- 2 cloves garlic, minced
- 1 tsp ginger, grated
- Wooden skewers, soaked in water

Preparation instructions:
1. Preheat the Ninja Dual Zone Air Fryer to 200°C for 5 minutes.
2. In a bowl, mix soy sauce, coconut milk, red curry paste, honey, lime juice, minced garlic, and grated ginger.
3. Thread chicken strips onto soaked wooden skewers and place them in one zone of the air fryer basket.
4. Brush the chicken skewers with the prepared marinade.
5. Air fry at 200°C for 12 minutes or until the chicken is cooked through and has a nice char.
6. Serve the Thai chicken satay skewers with additional lime wedges.

Cheddar and Chive Potato Skins

Serves: 4
Prep time: 15 minutes
Cook time: 20 minutes

Ingredients:
- 4 large potatoes, baked
- 100g cheddar cheese, shredded
- 2 tbsp chives, finely chopped
- Salt and black pepper, to taste
- Olive oil for brushing

Preparation instructions:
1. Preheat the Ninja Dual Zone Air Fryer to 200°C for 5 minutes.
2. Cut the baked potatoes in half lengthwise. Scoop out the flesh, leaving a thin layer.
3. Brush the potato skins with olive oil and place them in one zone of the air fryer basket.
4. In a bowl, mix shredded cheddar, chopped chives, salt, and black pepper.
5. Fill each potato skin with the cheddar and chive mixture.
6. Air fry at 200°C for 15 minutes or until the cheese is melted and bubbly.
7. Serve hot.

Courgette and Red Pepper Fritters

Serves: 4
Prep time: 15 minutes
Cook time: 10 minutes

Ingredients:
- 2 courgettes, grated
- 1 red pepper, finely diced
- 100g plain flour
- 2 large eggs
- 2 tbsp fresh parsley, chopped
- 1/2 tsp baking powder
- Salt and black pepper, to taste
- Olive oil for frying

Preparation instructions:
1. Preheat the Ninja Dual Zone Air Fryer to 180°C for 5 minutes.
2. In a bowl, combine grated courgettes, diced red pepper, plain flour, eggs, chopped parsley, baking powder, salt, and black pepper.
3. Mix until well combined.
4. Heat olive oil in a pan and drop spoonfuls of the mixture into the pan, flattening them slightly.
5. Fry for 2-3 minutes on each side until golden brown.
6. Transfer the fritters to one zone of the air fryer basket.
7. Air fry at 180°C for an additional 5 minutes to ensure they are fully cooked.
8. Serve warm.

Panko-Crusted Mozzarella Sticks with Marinara

Serves: 4
Prep time: 15 minutes
Cook time: 10 minutes

Ingredients:
- 200g mozzarella cheese, cut into sticks
- 100g panko breadcrumbs
- 2 large eggs, beaten
- 50g grated Parmesan cheese
- 1 tsp dried oregano
- 1/2 tsp garlic powder
- Salt and black pepper, to taste
- Marinara sauce for dipping

Preparation instructions:
1. Preheat the Ninja Dual Zone Air Fryer to 200°C for 5 minutes.
2. In one bowl, combine panko breadcrumbs, grated Parmesan, dried oregano, garlic powder, salt, and black pepper.
3. Dip each mozzarella stick into beaten eggs, then coat with the breadcrumb mixture.
4. Place the coated mozzarella sticks in one zone of the air fryer basket.
5. Air fry at 200°C for 8-10 minutes or until golden and crispy.
6. Serve with marinara sauce for dipping.

Spicy Sweet Potato and Chickpea Samosas

Serves: 4
Prep time: 20 minutes
Cook time: 15 minutes

Ingredients:
- 300g sweet potatoes, peeled and diced
- 200g canned chickpeas, drained and rinsed
- 1 onion, finely chopped
- 2 cloves garlic, minced
- 1 tsp ground cumin
- 1 tsp ground coriander
- 1/2 tsp turmeric
- 1/2 tsp chilli powder
- Salt and black pepper, to taste
- 200g filo pastry sheets
- 60ml olive oil

Preparation instructions:
1. Preheat the Ninja Dual Zone Air Fryer to 180°C for 5 minutes.
2. In a pan, boil sweet potatoes until tender. Mash them and set aside.
3. In another pan, sauté chopped onions and garlic until translucent.
4. Add chickpeas, cumin, coriander, turmeric, chilli powder, salt, and black pepper. Cook for 3-4 minutes.
5. Combine the chickpea mixture with mashed sweet potatoes.
6. Cut filo pastry sheets into squares. Spoon the filling onto each square.
7. Fold the pastry to create triangular samosas. Seal the edges with a bit of water.
8. Brush samosas with olive oil and place them in one zone of the air fryer basket.
9. Air fry at 180°C for 12-15 minutes or until golden brown.
10. Serve hot.

Bacon-Wrapped Jalapeño Poppers

Serves: 4
Prep time: 15 minutes
Cook time: 10 minutes

Ingredients:
- 8 large jalapeño peppers, halved and seeds removed
- 200g cream cheese
- 100g shredded cheddar cheese
- 8 slices streaky bacon
- 1 tsp smoked paprika
- Salt and black pepper, to taste

Preparation instructions:
1. Preheat the Ninja Dual Zone Air Fryer to 200°C for 5 minutes.
2. In a bowl, mix cream cheese, shredded cheddar, smoked paprika, salt, and black pepper.
3. Fill each jalapeño half with the cream cheese mixture.
4. Wrap each stuffed jalapeño with a slice of bacon, securing with toothpicks.
5. Place the bacon-wrapped jalapeños in one zone of the air fryer basket.
6. Air fry at 200°C for 10 minutes or until the bacon is crispy.
7. Remove toothpicks before serving.
8. Serve warm.

Spicy Cauliflower Bites with Blue Cheese Dip

Serves: 4
Prep time: 15 minutes
Cook time: 12 minutes

Ingredients:
- 500g cauliflower florets
- 30g grated Parmesan cheese
- 1/2 tsp garlic powder
- Salt and black pepper, to taste
- 60ml hot sauce
- 50g breadcrumbs
- 1 tsp smoked paprika
- 1/2 tsp onion powder
- 2 large eggs, beaten
- 60g unsalted butter, melted

Blue Cheese Dip:
- 150g Greek yoghurt
- 1 tbsp lemon juice
- 50g blue cheese, crumbled
- Salt and black pepper, to taste

Preparation instructions:
1. Preheat one zone of the Ninja Dual Zone Air Fryer to 200°C for 5 minutes.
2. In a bowl, mix breadcrumbs, Parmesan, smoked paprika, garlic powder, onion powder, salt, and black pepper.
3. Dip cauliflower florets into beaten eggs, then coat with the breadcrumb mixture.
4. Place the coated cauliflower in one zone of the air fryer basket.
5. Air fry at 200°C for 12 minutes or until golden brown and crispy.
6. In a separate bowl, mix Greek yoghurt, crumbled blue cheese, lemon juice, salt, and black pepper for the dip.
7. In the other zone of the air fryer basket, melt butter, add hot sauce, and mix.
8. Toss the air-fried cauliflower in the hot sauce mixture.
9. Serve the spicy cauliflower bites with the blue cheese dip.

Mini Pizza Parcels

Serves: 4
Prep time: 15 minutes
Cook time: 10 minutes

Ingredients:
- 1 sheet puff pastry, rolled and cut into strips
- 200g pizza sauce
- 150g shredded mozzarella cheese
- 50g sliced pepperoni
- 1 tsp dried oregano
- 1 tsp dried basil
- 1/2 tsp garlic powder

Preparation instructions:
1. Preheat the other zone of the Ninja Dual Zone Air Fryer to 200°C for 5 minutes.
2. Place puff pastry strips on a clean surface.
3. In the end of each strip, add pizza sauce, mozzarella, pepperoni, oregano, basil, and garlic powder.
4. Roll the pastry over the filling, creating neat rolls.
5. Place the pizza parcels in the other zone of the air fryer basket.
6. Air fry at 200°C for 10 minutes or until the parcels are golden brown.
7. Serve the mini pizza parcels warm.

CHAPTER 11
Sweet Snacks and Desserts

Cinnamon Sugar Apple Chips

Serves: 4
Prep time: 10 minutes
Cook time: 2 hours

Ingredients:
- 4 medium apples, thinly sliced
- 1 tbsp lemon juice
- 1 tsp ground cinnamon
- 2 tbsp granulated sugar

Preparation instructions:
1. Preheat one zone of the Ninja Dual Zone Air Fryer to 70°C for 5 minutes.
2. In a large bowl, toss the thinly sliced apples with lemon juice to prevent browning.
3. In a separate bowl, mix ground cinnamon and granulated sugar.
4. Sprinkle the cinnamon sugar mixture over the apple slices and toss to coat evenly.
5. Place the coated apple slices in one zone of the air fryer basket, ensuring they are not overlapping.
6. Air fry at 70°C for 2 hours, checking and flipping the slices halfway through.
7. Once the apple chips are crispy and golden brown, remove them from the air fryer and let them cool before serving.

Air-Fried Banana Fritters with Chocolate Drizzle

Serves: 4
Prep time: 15 minutes
Cook time: 10 minutes

Ingredients:
- 4 ripe bananas, mashed
- 1 tbsp granulated sugar
- 1/2 tsp ground cinnamon
- Vegetable oil for frying
- 120g all-purpose flour
- 1 tsp baking powder
- Pinch of salt

Chocolate Drizzle:
- 50g dark chocolate, chopped
- 2 tbsp unsalted butter

Preparation instructions:
1. Preheat the other zone of the Ninja Dual Zone Air Fryer to 180°C for 5 minutes.
2. In a bowl, combine mashed bananas, flour, sugar, baking powder, ground cinnamon, and a pinch of salt.
3. Heat vegetable oil in a pan over medium heat.
4. Drop spoonfuls of the banana batter into the hot oil and fry until golden brown on both sides.
5. Place the fried banana fritters in the other zone of the air fryer basket.
6. Air fry at 180°C for 10 minutes, turning halfway through.
7. In a microwave-safe bowl, melt dark chocolate and butter, stirring until smooth.
8. Drizzle the chocolate over the air-fried banana fritters and serve warm.

Mini Blueberry and Lemon Scones

Serves: 4
Prep time: 15 minutes
Cook time: 12 minutes

Ingredients:
- 200g self-raising flour
- 30g granulated sugar
- Zest of 1 lemon
- 80ml milk
- 50g unsalted butter, cold and cubed
- 1/2 tsp baking powder
- 100g fresh blueberries
- 1 tsp vanilla extract

Preparation instructions:
1. Preheat one zone of the Ninja Dual Zone Air Fryer to 200°C for 5 minutes.
2. In a large bowl, rub the cold butter into the flour until it resembles breadcrumbs.
3. Add sugar, baking powder, lemon zest, and fresh blueberries to the mixture, stirring gently.
4. In a separate bowl, combine milk and vanilla extract.
5. Pour the wet ingredients into the dry ingredients and mix until just combined.
6. Turn the dough out onto a floured surface and shape into a round.
7. Cut mini scones from the dough and place them in one zone of the air fryer basket.
8. Air fry at 200°C for 12 minutes or until the scones are golden brown.
9. Let the mini blueberry and lemon scones cool slightly before serving.

Raspberry Almond Turnovers

Serves: 4
Prep time: 15 minutes
Cook time: 12 minutes

Ingredients:
- 1 sheet of puff pastry (approx. 320g), thawed
- 100g fresh raspberries
- 50g almond meal
- 30g granulated sugar
- 1/2 tsp almond extract
- 1 egg, beaten (for egg wash)

Preparation instructions:
1. Preheat one zone of the Ninja Dual Zone Air Fryer to 180°C for 5 minutes.
2. In a bowl, mix together fresh raspberries, almond meal, granulated sugar, and almond extract.
3. Roll out the puff pastry and cut it into four squares.
4. Spoon the raspberry-almond mixture onto each square.
5. Fold the pastry over to create a triangle, sealing the edges.
6. Brush each turnover with beaten egg for a golden finish.
7. Place the turnovers in one zone of the air fryer basket.
8. Air fry at 180°C for 12 minutes or until the turnovers are puffed and golden.
9. Allow the Raspberry Almond Turnovers to cool slightly before serving.

Vanilla-Coconut Glazed Pineapple Rings

Serves: 4
Prep time: 10 minutes
Cook time: 8 minutes

Ingredients:
- 1 medium pineapple, peeled and cored, cut into rings
- 50g desiccated coconut
- 60ml coconut milk
- 2 tbsp granulated sugar
- 1 tsp vanilla extract

Preparation instructions:
1. Preheat the other zone of the Ninja Dual Zone Air Fryer to 200°C for 5 minutes.
2. In a shallow bowl, mix desiccated coconut, coconut milk, granulated sugar, and vanilla extract.
3. Dip each pineapple ring into the coconut mixture, ensuring both sides are coated.
4. Place the coated pineapple rings in the other zone of the air fryer basket.
5. Air fry at 200°C for 8 minutes or until the coconut coating is golden and crisp.
6. Remove the Vanilla-Coconut Glazed Pineapple Rings from the air fryer and let them cool before serving.

Chocolate-Dipped Strawberry Puff Pastry Bites

Serves: 4
Prep time: 15 minutes
Cook time: 10 minutes

Ingredients:
- 1 sheet of puff pastry (approx. 320g), thawed
- 100g fresh strawberries, hulled and halved
- 100g dark chocolate, melted
- Icing sugar for dusting (optional)

Preparation instructions:
1. Preheat one zone of the Ninja Dual Zone Air Fryer to 180°C for 5 minutes.
2. Roll out the puff pastry and cut it into small squares.
3. Place a strawberry half on each puff pastry square.
4. Fold the pastry over the strawberry, sealing the edges.
5. Place the strawberry-filled puff pastry bites in one zone of the air fryer basket.
6. Air fry at 180°C for 10 minutes or until the puff pastry is golden brown.
7. Dip each bite into melted dark chocolate and let them cool.
8. Optionally, dust with icing sugar before serving.

Maple Pecan Air-Fried Donut Holes

Serves: 4
Prep time: 15 minutes
Cook time: 10 minutes

Ingredients:
- 200g self-raising flour
- 50g caster sugar
- 60ml maple syrup
- 60ml whole milk
- 40g unsalted butter, melted
- 1 tsp vanilla extract
- 50g pecans, chopped
- Icing sugar for dusting (optional)

Preparation instructions:
1. Preheat one zone of the Ninja Dual Zone Air Fryer to 180°C for 5 minutes.
2. In a bowl, combine self-raising flour, caster sugar, maple syrup, whole milk, melted butter, vanilla extract, and chopped pecans.
3. Mix until a dough forms. Divide the dough into small portions and shape them into donut holes.
4. Place the donut holes in one zone of the air fryer basket.
5. Air fry at 180°C for 10 minutes or until the donut holes are golden brown and cooked through.
6. Optionally, dust with icing sugar before serving.

Lemon Curd Stuffed Filo Pastry Parcels

Serves: 4
Prep time: 15 minutes
Cook time: 12 minutes

Ingredients:
- 4 sheets of filo pastry
- 200g lemon curd
- 50g unsalted butter, melted
- Icing sugar for dusting (optional)

Preparation instructions:
1. Preheat the other zone of the Ninja Dual Zone Air Fryer to 180°C for 5 minutes.
2. Lay out a sheet of filo pastry, brush it with melted butter, and place another sheet on top.
3. Repeat until you have four layers. Cut the layered pastry into four squares.
4. Spoon 50g of lemon curd into the centre of each square.
5. Fold the pastry over to create a parcel, sealing the edges.
6. Place the lemon curd-filled filo parcels in the other zone of the air fryer basket.
7. Air fry at 180°C for 12 minutes or until the parcels are golden brown and crisp.
8. Optionally, dust with icing sugar before serving.

Oatmeal Raisin Cookie Energy Bites

Serves: 4
Prep time: 15 minutes
Cook time: 5 minutes

Ingredients:
- 150g rolled oats
- 50g almond butter
- 60ml honey
- 1/2 tsp vanilla extract
- 50g raisins
- 30g chopped nuts (e.g., almonds or walnuts)

Preparation instructions:
1. In a bowl, combine rolled oats, almond butter, honey, and vanilla extract.
2. Mix in raisins and chopped nuts until well combined.
3. Shape the mixture into small, bite-sized energy bites.
4. Place the energy bites in one zone of the Ninja Dual Zone Air Fryer basket.
5. Air fry at 180°C for 5 minutes and serve warm!

Mini Cherry Bakewell Tarts

Serves: 4
Prep time: 20 minutes
Cook time: 10 minutes

Ingredients:
- 1 sheet of ready-rolled puff pastry (about 320g)
- 100g cherry jam
- 50g ground almonds
- 50g icing sugar
- 1/2 tsp almond extract
- 60ml water
- Flaked almonds for garnish (optional)

Preparation instructions:
1. Preheat the other zone of the Ninja Dual Zone Air Fryer to 180°C for 5 minutes.
2. Cut the puff pastry into squares and press them into the silicone muffin cups in the air fryer basket.
3. In a bowl, mix together cherry jam, ground almonds, icing sugar, almond extract, and water.
4. Spoon the cherry almond mixture into each puff pastry cup.
5. Garnish with flaked almonds if desired.
6. Place the muffin cups in the air fryer basket.
7. Air fry at 180°C for 10 minutes or until the pastry is golden brown.
8. Once cooked, remove from the air fryer and let cool for a few minutes before serving.

INDEX

A

Air-Fried Banana Fritters with Chocolate Drizzle 75
Air-Fried Black Bean and Corn Quesadillas 43
Air-Fried Butter Bean and Tomato Casserole 45
Air-Fried Chicken and Vegetable Spring Rolls 64
Air-Fried Chicken and Waffle Sliders 60
Air-Fried Chicken Tikka Masala Skewers 15
Air-Fried Chickpea and Sweet Potato Tacos 48
Air-Fried Mac and Cheese Bites 62
Air-Fried Mushroom and Lentil Burgers 18
Air-Fried Vegetable Paella with Saffron Rice 22
Air-Fried Veggie Hash Browns Delight 10

B

Bacon-Wrapped Jalapeño Poppers 72
Baked Beans and Sausage Stuffed Peppers 62
Banana-Oat Pancake Bites with Yoghurt Drizzle 13
BBQ Pulled Pork Loaded Potato Skins 67
BBQ Pulled Pork Stuffed Sweet Potatoes 16
Black-Eyed Pea and Vegetable Patties 48

C

Cajun-Style Air-Fried Haddock Nuggets 24
Cajun-Style Red Beans and Rice Fritters 44
Cheddar and Chive Potato Skins 70
Cheddar and Onion Stuffed Mushrooms 65
Cheesy Beans on Toast Twists 10
Cheesy Cauliflower Bites with Yoghurt Dip 55
Cheesy Potato and Bacon Croquettes 60
Chilli Lime Grilled Salmon Patties 28
Chocolate-Dipped Strawberry Puff Pastry Bites 77
Cinnamon Sugar Apple Chips 75
Coconut-Crusted Haddock Bites with Pineapple Salsa 25
Courgette and Red Pepper Fritters 71
Cranberry and Thyme Stuffed Chicken Thighs 37
Crispy Air-Fried Bruschetta Bites 69
Crispy Air-Fried Bubble and Squeak Patties 9
Crispy Coconut-Crusted Shrimp with Mango Salsa 20
Crispy Garlic Parmesan Chicken Strips 61
Crispy Garlic Parmesan Edamame Snack 43
Crispy Rosemary and Garlic Fries 56
Crispy Tilapia with Dill Yoghurt Sauce 26
Crusted Mustard Pork Chops with Apple Compote 21
Cumin-Spiced Grilled Beef Kebabs 38
Cumin-Spiced Sweet Potato Wedges 53
Curried Lentil and Sweet Potato Bites 42
Curry-Spiced Squash Rings 58

E

English Muffin Egg Cups with Turkey Sausage 9

F

Family-Style Chicken and Veggie Quesadillas 64

G

Garlic Brussels Sprouts Chips 53
Garlic Butter Lemon and Herb Shrimp Skewers 24

H

Harissa-Spiced Chickpea Fries 46
Herb-Crusted Pork Loin 39
Herbed Breadcrumb-Crusted Cod Fillets 27
Herb-Roasted Butternut Squash Cubes 57
Hoisin Ginger Glazed Pork Belly Slices 37
Homemade Chicken Nuggets with Honey Mustard Dip 66
Honey Balsamic Glazed Beetroot Slices 56

J

Jerk Chicken Thighs with Mango Salsa 35

K

Kidney Bean and Vegetable Stuffed Mushrooms 47

L

Lemon and Herb Butter Basted Chicken Thighs 39

Lemon Curd Stuffed Filo Pastry Parcels 78
Lemon Dill Air-Fried Asparagus Spears 54
Lemon Herb Tinned Salmon Parcels with Veggies 15
Lemon Pepper Cod Bites 27

M
Maple Dijon Glazed Turkey Meatballs 35
Maple Pecan Air-Fried Donut Holes 78
Meatball Sub Skewers with Marinara Dipping Sauce 63
Mediterranean Chickpea Frittatas in the Air Fryer 13
Mediterranean Lamb Kofta Patties 36
Mediterranean Stuffed Calamari Rings 25
Mediterranean Stuffed Mushrooms with Quinoa 54
Mediterranean Stuffed Peppers with Quinoa 44
Mini Beef and Veggie Pies with Puff Pastry 61
Mini Blueberry and Lemon Scones 76
Mini Cherry Bakewell Tarts 79
Mini Pizza Parcels 73
Moroccan Spiced Lamb Meatballs 19
Moroccan Spiced Sea Bass Parcels 31
Mushroom and Tomato Breakfast Quesadillas 12

N
Ninja Dual Zone Full English Breakfast Bites 11

O
Oatmeal Raisin Cookie Energy Bites 79

P
Panko-Crusted Falafel Nuggets 45
Panko-Crusted Mozzarella Sticks with Marinara 71
Paprika-Rubbed Air-Fried Pork Tenderloin 34
Parmesan Courgette Crisps with Basil Dip 52
Pesto Crusted Cod with Roasted Vegetables 17
Pesto Marinated Grilled Chicken Skewers 36
Pesto Parmesan Aubergine Slices 55

R
Raspberry Almond Turnovers 76
Ratatouille-Stuffed Peppers 20
Rosemary and Garlic Air-Fried Lamb Chops 33

S
Sausage and Pea Pastry Parcels 66
Sesame Crusted Tuna Steaks with Wasabi Mayo 30
Sesame Soy Air-Fried Broccoli Bites 51
Smoked Paprika Prawn Tacos 26
Smoky BBQ Baked Beans with Bacon 46
Spiced Apricot Glazed Chicken Breast 34
Spiced Carrot and Chickpea Fritters 52
Spicy Cauliflower Bites with Blue Cheese Dip 73
Spicy Chickpea and Spinach Air-Fried Patties 42
Spicy Harissa Marinated Grilled Shrimp 29
Spicy Sweet Potato and Chickpea Samosas 72
Spinach and Feta Stuffed Mushrooms 11
Spinach and Feta Stuffed Portobello Mushrooms 21
Spinach and Mozzarella Stuffed Mushrooms 69
Spinach and Ricotta-Stuffed Chicken Breasts 16
Sticky Honey Mustard Chicken Drumsticks 33
Sweet and Sour Chicken Stir-Fry 63
Sweet Potato Rosti with Avocado Smash 12

T
Tandoori Spiced Chicken Wings 40
Teriyaki Glazed Salmon Skewers with Bok Choy 30
Teriyaki Glazed Tofu with Sesame Broccoli 19
Teriyaki Pineapple Turkey Burgers 38
Thai Chicken Satay Skewers 70
Thai-Inspired Basil Chicken Stir-Fry 18
Thai Red Curry Mussels in the Air Fryer 28
Tomato Basil Caprese Stuffed Sweet Potatoes 57
Turmeric and Cumin-Spiced Lentil Chips 47
Turmeric Roasted Cauliflower Steaks 51

V
Vanilla-Coconut Glazed Pineapple Rings 77
Vegan Chickpea and Vegetable Kebabs 17
Veggie-Packed Air-Fried Chicken Burgers 65

W
Warm Herbed Cannellini Bean Salad 49

Z
Zesty Tandoori Grilled Tuna Steaks 29

Printed in Great Britain
by Amazon